ACTS OF WORSHIP

A *Lillenas* DRAMA RESOURCE

ACTS OF WORSHIP

Dramatic Devotionals for Drama People

by
Jeff Wyatt and Paul M. Miller

Authors of *The Word in Worship*

Lillenas PUBLISHING COMPANY

KANSAS CITY, MO 64141

Dedication

I dedicate my efforts toward this book to my wife, Debbie, and our daughter, Brianna, for their longsuffering, trust, and inspiration.

—J.W.

And, I . . . to Tim and Lisa for whom worship has always been a "verb."

—P.M.M.

Contents

Acts of Worship: **Scripture Arrangements**

Preface

There are rehearsals and then there are rehearsals. Whoever dreamed up the old bad-rehearsal-good-performance adage never directed a church drama group. Bad rehearsals spawn bad performances. Period.

"Well, then, how do you insure a good rehearsal?"

Fair question. I'm not sure how to insure it, but I do know that when it happens there is usually a good mix of preparation, focus, concentration, humor, and sense of ministry. And, how does the director insure that all of these rehearsal attributes will be present? There is no way it can be insured, but you know when it happens.

For years our drama group went the route of less-than-desirable rehearsals.

"Whoa, be honest. We had some real doggy rehearsals. Why, I remember one time when you . . ."

Never mind. This isn't a history lesson, it's a handbook on how a creative devotional time can prepare cast and crew for better than usual rehearsals.

Just a few years ago I felt our Kansas City First Drama Ensemble group needed a fresh vision of purpose and ministry. We'd become reasonably successful and, as our egos led us to believe, we'd be successful with just about anything we undertook.

While we began most meetings and rehearsals with prayer and some so-called sharing (which often consisted of a recounting of the day's trials and tribulations), the exercise did not energize us for a rehearsal or an acting class.

Then came the dawn. During the two-month rehearsal schedule for a major production, which always includes Saturday morning rehearsals, and during our season of Wednesday evening drama meetings, we'd spend 15 to 20 minutes in an energetic devotional that would involve the group as participants and would provide plenty of opportunity for sharing and prayer.

"Sometimes it lasted longer than 15 minutes."

All right, sometimes we went longer. But 15 to 20 minutes was our goal.

"Just trying to keep you honest."

Thank you.

In the early stages of these enhanced devotional periods, my writing partner Jeff Wyatt was in charge. One year when we were rehearsing three one-acts for dinner theatre, our Saturday morning practice concentrated on Dale Wasserman's charming 1840s play *Shining Mountains.* It's all about Indians and fur trappers, a missionary couple, and an orphan boy.

While we munched on potluck breakfast, Jeff informed us about Paiutes and beaver pelts and the hardships of Western expansion. Then he'd shift gears and the first thing we knew, we were involved in a scripted Scripture lesson or other spiritual exercise, which woke us up and got us ready for an intelligent rehearsal.

During the off season, when we'd meet for Wednesday evening acting classes and script reading, Jeff continued the 15- to 20-minute devotionals, this time around drama and theatre themes, some of which are represented in this collection. Today, members of the group are continuing the devotional tradition.

Acts of Worship is a devotional resource for your drama group or for any group that wants to bring life and light to those minutes spent in the Word. Saturate its ideas with your imagination. Adapt its concepts to better complement your purpose. Use these pages as a model in writing your own material.

PAUL M. MILLER
Lillenas Drama

A Word About This Book

Drama is an effective aid to worship. If this assertion does not sound completely foreign, it is because we are enjoying a period in church history in which a growing number of Christians are utilizing drama in worship and outreach. For too many years, drama as a means of celebrating God's presence and communicating the gospel was ignored by many Christians.

The return of drama to Christian worship should not be too surprising. After all, we serve a creative God who has gifted each of us with creativity. Offering our human creativity to God and to others celebrates and glorifies the God who created us. Scripture itself is filled with the same elements that make drama entertaining and enriching—creativity, imagination, story, character. When these elements are identified in Scripture and used carefully and intentionally, drama becomes a powerful tool for communicating the content and character of the Christian faith.

This is not to say that *everyone* is anxiously anticipating the return of drama to Christian worship. Historically, drama has often been a vital part of worship and education in the church, but the use of drama in worship has always been surrounded by a certain amount of tension. The tension between drama and worship is healthy. The absence of this tension is what should concern us. One way to erase the tension is to ignore drama, but ignoring our gifts does not glorify God or edify the community. The other way to erase the tension is to reduce worship in favor of drama, but drama is not a substitute for worship. Neither of these solutions is acceptable, so we must learn to live with a certain amount of tension between drama and worship.

We live with the tension between drama and worship by centering drama ministry in the church around a covenant. The ministry covenant is a call to realize the implications of the gifts, given by God, to effect drama ministry in the church. The covenant is a way of focusing drama ministry on the community it is called to serve. The ministry covenant also reminds the participants in drama ministry of their vulnerability and their need to support each other.

The devotionals that follow were written to nurture a sense of covenant among those involved in drama ministry. They are also intended to illustrate the conviction that drama really is an effective aid to worship. You will notice an emphasis on participation. We hope that as you celebrate God's presence together, even for 10 minutes or less, that you will be reminded of your commitment to one another and to ministry.

Finally, although the following devotionals can be informative, they were designed primarily to pull you and your drama group into a dialogue with the Word. So, after reading through one of these devotionals, we hope you will not be too concerned if you do not "get it." After all, the point of these worship exercises is to remind us of God's presence, and in the presence of God we do not need so much to "get it" as to let God "get us."

JEFF WYATT

Acts of Worship:

Character Interpretations

The devotionals in this first section are based upon very familiar biblical characters and events. As you peruse these pages, you will discover that they are written as readers theatre, with participation opportunity for the total group. This will necessitate photocopying scripts, which is permissible.

Some of the scripts have devotional activities suggested throughout. All of them have a group dynamic, improv situation, or acting game suggested at the close. These will supply group involvement and should prepare the participants for an upbeat rehearsal or study group.

Yes, I see that hand.

"Uh, I'd like to use some of these devotionals with my Bible study group. Will that work?"

Go to it! Yes?

"Do you think we could perform these readers theatre pieces in a Sunday church service?"

I plan to.

Now, enough chitchat, let's get to work.

13

David 1: God Has a Purpose

Scripture: 1 Samuel 16:1-13

Theme: God is more concerned about the heart than with outward appearance.

Cast: Leader, God, Samuel, Group, Jesse, Ozem, David

Part 1

LEADER: One day the Lord spoke to Samuel, who was grieved over the moral failure of Saul, the king of Israel.

GOD: How long are you going to mourn for Saul, brother Samuel?

SAMUEL: I don't know, Lord. It's all so . . .

GOD *(interrupting):* I know how you feel, Samuel. I am grieved that I ever made him king over Israel, but we have to try again.

SAMUEL: What do you mean, Lord?

GOD: I mean, we have to find a replacement for Saul.

SAMUEL: Where are we going to start looking, Lord?

GOD: I have already found him, Samuel.

SAMUEL: Oh, really?

GOD: That's right.

SAMUEL: Who, Lord?

GOD: I am sending you to Jesse of Bethlehem . . .

SAMUEL *(interrupting):* Ah, he's awfully old, isn't he, Lord?

GOD: Not Jesse, Samuel. I have selected one of his sons.

SAMUEL: Which one, Lord?

GOD: That is for you to find out, Samuel.

SAMUEL: Me?

GOD: That's right.

SAMUEL *(fearfully):* But how can I go, Lord? Saul will hear about it and have me killed.

GOD: I have a plan.

SAMUEL *(tinge of sarcasm):* Oh, great.

GOD *(ignoring him):* You need to take a heifer to Bethlehem with you, and when folks ask what you are doing in Bethlehem, you can say, "I have come to make sacrifice to the Lord." Got that, Samuel?

SAMUEL: I think so.

GOD: Good.

SAMUEL: But what does this have to do with Jesse?

GOD: You will invite Jesse and his boys to participate in the sacrifice.

SAMUEL: Then what?

GOD: Never mind now. I will let you know the next step in due time.

SAMUEL: Why is it, Lord, that I always have to start out on some mission for you without knowing how it'll end up?

GOD: Take it as a compliment, Samuel. Now, fill your horn with oil and be on your way.

Part 2

LEADER: Samuel did as the Lord directed. When he arrived in Bethlehem with the heifer in tow, he was met by the town elders.

GROUP *(nervously):* Ah, Samuel, welcome to Bethlehem. Do you come in peace?

SAMUEL: Of course I come in peace. How else?

GROUP: So why have you come to our fair city?

SAMUEL: Why, I have come to . . . to . . .

GROUP: Yes?

SAMUEL: Why, I have come to make sacrifice to the Lord. Yes, that's it!

GROUP *(letting out their breath with relief):* Good.

LEADER: Then Samuel spied Jesse with seven of his sons. He took them to one side . . .

SAMUEL *(under his breath):* Jesse, will you join me in making sacrifice?

JESSE: Sure, Samuel. Me and the boys would be pleased, but we'll need to go by the house to get cleaned up first.

LEADER: So Samuel, Jesse, and the seven boys went out to the farm, where they dutifully bathed and put on clean clothes for the sacrifice.

Part 3

LEADER: During the rite of consecration, Samuel studied each of the seven sons of Jesse.

SAMUEL *(to himself):* One of these strapping young men will be the next king of Israel, but which one will it be?

JESSE: Have you met my sons, Samuel? This is my eldest, Eliab.

SAMUEL *(to himself with confidence):* Surely this sturdy young man standing here before me is the Lord's anointed.

LEADER: But in a voice heard only by Samuel, the Lord replied . . .

GOD *(quietly):* Now, Samuel, don't let his striking appearance influence you. He is not the one.

LEADER: Then the Lord added . . .

GOD *(still quietly):* We went that way before with Saul. Remember, humans look at the outward appearance, but I look at the heart.

JESSE: And this is my second son, he is Abinadab.

GOD: No, Samuel, I have not chosen this one either.

JESSE: Well, you might as well meet the rest of the family, Samuel. Come on over here, boys. This is Shammah, and here is Nathaniel, and those three are Raddai, Ozem, and Zeruiah.

GOD: No, Samuel, none of these men are my choice for king of Israel. You might ask if there isn't another boy in the family.

SAMUEL: Well, Jesse, I'm really pleased to meet your boys like this, but you know, I always thought you had eight boys.

JESSE: I do! But my youngest isn't much, he's out in the pasture tending my sheep.

SAMUEL: Send for him, please, Jesse. I want to meet him too.

JESSE: Ah, Samuel, you don't want to see him, he'll be a mess.

SAMUEL: That's all right, Jesse. The Lord and I want to see his heart.

LEADER: So Ozem went off to the north pasture to find his kid brother, totally oblivious to what was about to transpire.

Part 4

GROUP *(making sheep noises):* Baaaa.

OZEM *(calling):* David, is that you over there? *(No answer)* David, we have company, and Dad wants you to come to the house right now.

DAVID *(from a distance):* Wait a minute, Ozem, I'm just finishing up a new sheep song.

OZEM: David, I think you best come now! The company is Samuel—and you know how Dad is when a preacher comes to call.

DAVID *(coming closer):* Oh, all right, Ozem. Say, got any ideas of what rhymes with "green pastures"?

OZEM: I don't know, David. And I sure don't know why Samuel wants to see a strange one like you.

Part 5

JESSE: Say, here they are now. Samuel was just asking about you, David.

LEADER: So Samuel sized David up one side and down the other, conscious, of course, that God looks at the heart.

SAMUEL *(to himself):* Well, he's a ruddy and handsome young fellow. What about it, Lord?

GOD *(quietly):* Yes, he makes a fine appearance, Samuel, but better than that, he has strength of character.

SAMUEL: So, what shall I do, Lord?

GOD: Stand and anoint him king!

LEADER: So Samuel took the horn of oil and anointed David in the presence of his father and seven brothers.

SAMUEL: From this day on, O future King David, the Spirit of God is upon you.

*   *   *   *   *

A Devotional Improv

Print the following improv dialogues/situations on 3" x 5" cards and give to person taking part. Each should be presented in some character devised by the participant. They may involve others in the group as they wish. Allow a five-minute prep period.

- "Well, George, my way of knowing God's will for my life is . . ."
- "The indications of a 'good' heart are . . ."
- "Whataya mean, I'm too young to . . ."
- Recite Psalm 23 as if the writer were a football player and not a shepherd.
- "So how does God talk to you? Do you hear a voice?"
- With another person representing David, mime Samuel's reaction to David coming in from the sheepfold, and then anointing him.

David 2:
How to Be a Giant Killer

Scripture: 1 Samuel 17:1-58

Theme: You can't defeat the enemy in someone else's armor.

Cast: Leader, Samuel, Servant 1, Servant 2, Servant 3, Saul, David, Goliath, Eliab, Group

---

LEADER: The small circle of witnesses to David's anointing assured its confidentiality until Saul was replaced as king.

SAMUEL: Now the Spirit of the Lord had departed from Saul, and an evil spirit tormented him.

LEADER: Saul's court knew their king was tormented.

SERVANT 1: My Lord, let us find someone who can play the harp and soothe you when the evil spirit comes upon you.

SAUL: So be it. Find someone—and do it quickly!

SERVANT 2: I have seen one of Jesse's sons playing a harp out in his father's sheep pasture.

SAUL: One of Jesse's boys? Which one?

SERVANT 2: The small one who sings to sheep.

SAUL: But what kind of a fellow is he?

SERVANT 3: He sings and speaks well and he's a fine-looking young man. I believe the Lord is with him.

SAUL: Then go and bring him here at once; I feel a torment coming on.

LEADER: So David was brought to Saul and entered his service. The king liked him very much. After a few weeks Saul made a point of seeking out the shepherd boy.

SAUL: You please me very much, David. Every time I feel a torment coming on, and you sing—well, it makes me feel much better. I want to reward your good service by making you my armor-bearer.

DAVID: Well, thank you, sir. The Lord gives me the songs I sing, and all I know about harp playing I learned in the north pasture—that's how I used to calm my father's sheep when they got tormented.

Saul: I will ignore that you just likened me to your father's sheep.

David: Thank you, sir. Sir?

Saul: Yes, David?

David: What is an armor-bearer?

Leader: It wasn't long before David found out. The Philistines were gathering their forces for war against Israel. When the day of battle came, the Philistines occupied one hill and the Israelites another, with the valley between them. In his tent, Saul paced and contemplated the battle.

Saul: They have a champion warrior named Goliath from Gath. He's over nine feet tall; he wears a bronze helmet and a coat of armor that weighs 5,000 shekels. On his legs he wears bronze shin guards and carries a javelin that's the size of a weaver's rod with an iron point that weighs 600 shekels.

Leader: The next day when morning broke, Goliath stood on his hilltop and shouted across the valley . . .

Goliath: Come on out and line up for battle, you Israelites. Choose a man and have him come down to me. If he is able to fight and kill me, we will become your subjects.

Leader: Meanwhile, back in Bethlehem, old Jesse was preparing a care package to send to his sons at the front. He called David home to deliver it.

Jesse: David, I want you to take this sack of roasted grain and these loaves of bread to your brothers at their camp, and these cheeses too. Be quick about it. I want some assurance that they're all right.

Leader: So early in the morning David left his sheep and set out to the Valley of Elah. He reached the camp just as the army was going out to take its battle positions shouting the battle cry . . .

Saul: Give me an "I"!

Group: "I"!

Saul: Give me an "S"!

Group: "S"!

Saul: Give me an "R"!

Group: "R"!

Saul: Give me an "A"!

Group: "A"!

SAUL: Give me an "E"!

GROUP: "E"!

SAUL: Give me an "L"!

GROUP: "L"!

SAUL: Put them together and what do you have?

GROUP: Israel! Israel! Israel! Yeahhhh!

LEADER: As David was talking to his brothers, behold, Goliath, the Philistine champion from Gath stepped out from his lines and shouted his usual defiance.

GOLIATH: Come on, you Israelites, choose a man and have him come down to do battle with me!

LEADER: Well, when the Israelites saw the man, they all ran from him in great fear, but not David. The young man turned to one standing by and asked,

DAVID: Who is this unclean Philistine that he should defy the armies of the living God?

LEADER: Now, when Eliab, David's oldest brother, heard him speaking to the men, he burned with anger and asked,

ELIAB: Why have you come down here, David? And who did you leave the sheep with? I know how conceited you are and how wicked your heart is; you came down here for sport—just to watch the battle.

LEADER: Word soon got to Saul that David was on the battlefield and acting as if he was not afraid of Goliath. So the king sent for David. When David presented himself to Saul, he proclaimed,

DAVID: Let no one lose heart on account of this Philistine; I will go and fight him!

SAUL: David, you are not able to go out and fight him; you are only a boy.

DAVID: My lord, I have been taking good care of my father's sheep. When a lion or a bear came to our camp, and carried off a sheep from the flock, I went after it, struck it, and rescued the sheep from its mouth. Whenever a lion or bear turned on me, I seized it by its hair, struck it, and killed it. I have killed both a lion and a bear single-handed. Why should I be afraid of this Philistine?

LEADER: With that, all Saul could say was,

SAUL: Go, David, and the Lord be with you. But first, let me dress you for battle.

DAVID: But I'm fine just as I am, king.

SAUL: No, here, put on this tunic. Now, this is my personal coat of armor and bronze helmet. They will serve you well.

LEADER: Then David fastened on his sword and tried to walk around.

DAVID: I can't go to battle in this getup. Here, let me get out of them. Just give me my shepherd's staff, my sling, and five smooth stones.

LEADER: Meanwhile, Goliath and his shield bearer moved closer to David. He carefully looked the lad over and saw how handsome and ruddy he was, but they saw he was only a boy.

GOLIATH: Am I a dog, little boy, that you come at me with sticks? By my gods, I'll give your flesh to the birds of the air and the beasts of the field.

DAVID: You come against me with sword and spear, but I come against you in the name of the Lord Almighty, the God of the armies of Israel, whom you have defiled. All those gathered here today will know that it is not by sword or spear that the Lord saves; for the battle is the Lord's.

LEADER: With that, David reached into his shepherd's pouch and took out a stone, placed it in the sling, and fired away at the giant Philistine.

DAVID: In the name of the God of Israel, take this!

LEADER: The smooth stone from David's sling found its mark—Goliath's forehead.

GROUP: Look at Goliath, the giant Philistine, like a mighty tree, he has fallen!

SAUL: David has triumphed over the Philistine with a sling and a stone; without a sword in his hand he struck down the giant and killed him.

LEADER: As Saul watched David, he said to Abner, the commander of his army,

SAUL: Whose son is that young man?

LEADER: So Abner went to David and brought him before his king.

SAUL: Young man, whose son are you?

LEADER: And David answered with great truth and simplicity,

DAVID: I, David, am the son of your servant Jesse of Bethlehem.

Acting Out Your Faith

Use some of these activities to help the group relate this familiar Old Testament story to their worlds.

- Read Ephesians 6:11 ("Put on the full armor of God . . .") and improvise a soldier getting dressed in his armor and talking about what each piece represents.
- Improvise a monologue by David while he's wearing Saul's armor.

- Improvise an imaginary conversation about the difference in size between Goliath and David.

- Select a partner who will interview you, as David, regarding how you felt when you stood alone on the battlefield with Goliath. How did David's faith in God see him through the battle.

- Perhaps some in the group will want to share some of the "Goliaths" in their lives. You may want to close in prayer for these giant situations.

- Devise a monologue in which David tells why he selected "five smooth stones."

David 3: Winning Friends and Influencing People

Scripture: 1 Samuel 18:1-29

Theme: Jealousy

Cast: Leader, Saul, Officer, Women, David, Group, Men

Part 1

LEADER: From the day David killed Goliath, Saul kept David with him and did not let him return to his father's house.

SAUL: That David is an unusual young man. Whatever I tell him to do, he does it—successfully!

OFFICER: Are you going to reward his service, sire?

SAUL: I think I'll give him a high rank in my army. That should show him how pleased I am with him.

LEADER: That pleased all the people, and Saul's officers too.

GROUP: Two, four, six, eight; who do we appreciate? Saul! Saul! Saul!

LEADER: When the men returned home after David had killed the big Philistine, the women came out from all the towns of Israel to meet King Saul with singing and dancing.

WOMEN: Saul has slain his thousands.

GROUP: Hooray for King Saul!

WOMEN: And David has slain his tens of thousands.

GROUP: Hooray for David!

SAUL *(suspiciously):* What are those women singing?

WOMEN: Saul has slain his thousands,

SAUL: and what has David done?

WOMEN: David has slain his tens of thousands.

SAUL *(angrily):* They have credited David with tens of thousands, but me with only thousands. What more can he get but the kingdom? I believe I had best keep my eye on him.

LEADER: From that time on Saul kept a jealous eye on David.

Part 2

LEADER: The next day, while David was playing his harp, Saul took his spear in hand . . .

GROUP *(whispering):* Look out, David!

SAUL: I'll pin David to the wall!

GROUP *(yelling):* Look out, David!

SAUL *(throwing spear):* Take this, you traitor!

LEADER: Twice the king tried to impale the young man on his spear; twice David eluded him.

SAUL *(to himself):* I must get rid of David. His successes frighten me. *(Cunningly)* Perhaps if I send him away . . .

LEADER: So Saul sent David away and gave him command over a thousand men.

MEN *(chanting):* David . . . David . . . David!

LEADER: Everything that David put his hand to turned out to be a success.

DAVID: Any success I have comes from the Lord, who is with me.

SAUL *(to himself):* Your success frightens me, David.

LEADER: When Saul realized that the Lord was with David, Saul became all the more afraid of him, and he remained his enemy all the rest of his days.

Shakespeare and the Group on Jealousy

Othello is Shakespeare's monumental drama that deals with jealousy—while not deserved (read the play or rent the video), it is still every bit as damning to the soul and spirit. While no one in the group may be destined for the classic stage, encourage all who would like to orally interpret these lines from the Immortal Bard.

> *O! beware, my lord, of jealousy;*
> *It is the green-ey'd monster which doth mock*
> *The meat it feeds on; that cuckold lives in bliss*
> *Who, certain of his fate, loves not his wronger;*
> *But, O! what damned minutes tells he o'er*
> *Who dotes, yet doubts; suspects, yet soundly loves!* (III,3)

25

Jealousy cloaks itself in all kinds of disguises. No one wants to admit to the "green-eyed monster," but it can be part of a drama group like yours. Take a few moments to discuss how to guard against problem interpersonal relationships. How can each member of your group contribute to a spirit of self-correction. If the mood allows, invite participants to express support for other members in the group.

Isaiah: Experiencing God

Scripture: Isaiah 6:1-8

Theme: Preparation for ministry

Cast: Person 1 (Isaiah), Person 2, Person 3, Person 4, Group

PERSON 1: In the year that King Uzziah died, I, Isaiah, saw the Lord seated on a throne, high and lifted up, and the train of his robe filled the temple.

PERSON 2: Fact—The prophet Isaiah was a scribe in the royal palace in Jerusalem.

PERSON 3: Fact—He served God through the reign of five kings.

PERSON 4: But it was at the death of King Uzziah that Isaiah was called to special service.

PERSON 2: Fact—King Uzziah reigned from 792 to 740 B.C.

PERSON 3: Fact—He was a godly and powerful ruler.

PERSON 4: This is the vision God gave Isaiah.

PERSON 2: This is how God prepared his prophet for service.

PERSON 1: I saw the Lord . . . above him were seraphs . . .

PERSON 2: Fact—Seraphs were angelic beings.

PERSON 1: Each seraph had six wings: with two they covered their faces, with two they covered their feet, and with two they were flying.

PERSON 3: These angelic beings covered their eyes because they could not look directly at the glory of God.

PERSON 1: And these heavenly seraphs were calling to one another.

GROUP: Holy, holy, holy is the Lord Almighty; the whole earth is full of his glory.

PERSON 2: At the sound of their voices the doorposts and thresholds shook and the temple was filled with smoke.

PERSON 2: The power of God's voice could bring awe and terror.

PERSON 1: I saw the Lord . . . and cried, "Woe is me."

GROUP: "Woe is me."

PERSON 1: For I am a man of unclean lips, and I live among a people of unclean lips.

ALL: We are people of unclean lips.

PERSON 2: When you stand before God . . .

PERSON 3: When you encounter God . . .

PERSON 4: When you are confronted by God . . .

GROUP: We will say with Isaiah . . .

PERSON 1: My eyes have seen the King!

GROUP: The Lord Almighty.

PERSON 1: And, woe is me.

PERSON 2: Then one of the seraphs flew to the prophet with a live coal in his hand, which he had taken with tongs from the altar.

PERSON 1: With the coal he touched my mouth and said,

PERSON 4: See, this has touched your lips; your guilt is taken away and your sin atoned for.

PERSON 1: Then I heard the voice of the Lord saying,

PERSON 3: Whom shall I send? And who will go for us?

PERSON 1: And I said, "Here am I. Send me!"

GROUP: Fact—Today, God still prepares us for service.

A Devotional Exercise

● Improvise a conversation between King Uzziah and Isaiah, in which the prophet tells the king what happened to him in the Temple the year the monarch died.

● Turn to Isaiah 35. Read it as a description of the result of the prophet's vision of God. The language of the 10 verses is graphic and suggests dramatic movement. Assign each verse to a different participant and ask each to mime the verse's content or message.

● Spend some moments in serious meditation. Ask yourselves . . .

   ★ Am I spiritually prepared to be part of this drama ministry?

   ★ Do I have regular times in my life when I prayerfully stand before God and allow Him to speak to me?

   ★ Can people recognize that I have been with God?

★ Have I had a instance in my ministry that I can interpret as God's blessing upon what I am trying to do for Him?

Spend time in silent prayer about the results of these questions.

Daniel: A Resolve That Changed History

Scripture: Daniel 1

Theme: Personal standards

Cast: Leader, Men, Women, Male Reader 1, Male Reader 2, Female Reader, Group

---

LEADER: In the third year of the reign of Jehoiakim king of Judah, Nebuchadnezzar king of Babylon

GROUP: came to Jerusalem and besieged it.

LEADER: And the Lord delivered Jehoiakim king of Judah into his hand,

WOMEN: along with some of the articles from the temple of God.

MEN: These he carried off to the temple of his god in Babylonia

GROUP: and he put them in the treasure house of his god.

LEADER: Then the king ordered the chief of his court officials . . .

MALE READER 1: Bring in some of the Israelites from the royal court and the nobility.

MEN: Young men without any physical defect,

FEMALE READER: handsome,

WOMEN: showing aptitude for every kind of learning,

MEN: well informed, quick to understand,

GROUP: and qualified to serve in the king's palace.

LEADER: He was to teach them the language and literature of the Babylonians.

FEMALE READER: The king assigned them a daily amount of food and wine from the king's table.

MALE READER 2: They were to be trained for three years,

GROUP: and after that, they were to enter the king's service.

LEADER: Among these were some from Judah:

Women: Daniel,

Men: Hananiah,

Women: Mishael,

Men: and Azariah.

Leader: The chief official gave the young Hebrew men Babylonian names:

Male Reader 1: He named Daniel,

Group: Belteshazzar;

Female Reader: He named Hananiah,

Group: Shadrach;

Male Reader 2: He named Mishael,

Group: Meshach;

Female Reader: And he named Azariah,

Group: Abednego.

Leader: But Daniel resolved not to defile himself with the royal food and wine.

Male Reader 1: Chief official, I am Daniel and I have something to say. Please give me permission not to defile myself by eating the king's food and drinking the king's wine.

Leader: Now God caused the official to show favor and sympathy to Daniel, but he replied,

Male Reader 2: Daniel, I am afraid of my lord the king, who has assigned your food and drink.

Male Reader 1: But . . .

Male Reader 2 : Why should he see you looking worse than the other young men your age?

Male Reader 1: But . . .

Male Reader 2: The king would then have my head because of you.

Leader: Daniel then said to the guard whom the chief official had appointed over

Group: Daniel,

Men: Hananiah,

Women: Mishael,

GROUP: and Azariah,

MALE READER 1: Please test your servants for ten days . . .

MEN: Ten days?

MALE READER 1: Yes, ten days: Give us nothing but vegetables to eat and water to drink.

WOMEN: Vegetables and water?

MALE READER 1: That's right. Then compare our appearance with that of the young men who eat the royal food. Then treat your servants in accordance with what you see.

MALE READER 2: So be it! Guards, take away the choice food and bring in vegetables and water. We will test them for ten days.

LEADER: At the end of the ten days Daniel and his three friends looked healthier and better nourished than any of the young men who ate the royal food. When the chief official saw this he declared,

MALE READER 2: So be it! Guards, take away the choice food and bring in vegetables and water.

LEADER: At the end of the time set by the king, the chief official brought in the young men and presented them to Nebuchadnezzar.

FEMALE READER: The king talked with them and found none equal to

GROUP: Daniel,

MEN: Hananiah,

WOMEN: Mishael,

GROUP: and Azariah.

LEADER: So, the four young men entered the king's service.

FEMALE READER: And it was known far and wide that

MALE READER 1: in every matter of wisdom and understanding about which the king questioned them,

MALE READER 2: he found them ten times better than all the magicians and enchanters in his whole kingdom.

GROUP: Remember these words: Daniel resolved not to defile himself!

Deliberating Daniel's Dilemma

The story of Daniel's resolve has been part of most person's Christian education. So it's probable that its familiarity has dulled the keen edge of truth. After reading the foregoing script as a group, allow yourselves to contemporize this historical situation. You as leader may want to assume the role of some eastern European despot and make some pronouncement to members in the circle. Goad them into dialogue.

At some point bring the contemporizing closer to home. Ask a couple of people to assume the "despot" role, based on their real worlds. Perhaps an office manager who is threatened if he or she goes out "to unwind" after hours with fellow office workers. How does one resolve that?

Shadrach, Meshach, and Abednego: Firefighters

Scripture: Daniel 3

Theme: Standing for what's right

Cast: Narrator 1, Narrator 2, Narrator 3, Herald, Astrologer 1, Astrologer 2, Nebuchadnezzar, Shadrach, Meshach, Abednego

---

NARRATOR 1: King Nebuchadnezzar made an image of gold, ninety feet high and nine feet wide, and set it up on the plain of Dura in the province of Babylon.

NARRATOR 2: He then summoned the satraps, prefects, governors, advisers, treasurers, judges, magistrates and all the other provincial officials to come to the dedication of the image he had set up.

NARRATOR 3: So the satraps, prefects, governors, advisers, treasurers, judges, magistrates and all other provincial officials assembled for the dedication of the image that King Nebuchadnezzar had set up, and they stood before it.

NARRATOR 1: Then the Herald loudly proclaimed,

HERALD: This is what you are commanded to do, O peoples, nations and men of every language: As soon as you hear the sound of the horn *(optional bell ring)*, flute *(music)*, zither *(music)*, lyre *(music)*, harp *(music)*, pipes *(music)* and all kinds of music, you must fall down and worship the image of gold that King Nebuchadnezzar has set up. Whoever does not fall down and worship will immediately be thrown into a blazing furnace.

NARRATOR 1: Therefore, as soon as they heard the sound of the horn *(music)*, flute *(music)*, zither *(music)*, lyre *(music)*, harp *(music)*, pipes *(music)* and all kinds of music, all the peoples, nations and men of every language fell down and worshiped the image of gold that King Nebuchadnezzar had set up.

NARRATOR 2: At this time some astrologers came forward and denounced the Jews.

NARRATOR 3: They said to King Nebuchadnezzar,

ASTROLOGER 1: O king, live forever!

ASTROLOGER 2: You have issued a decree, O king, that everyone who hears the sound of the horn *(music)*, flute *(music)*, . . .

ASTROLOGER 1: zither *(music)*, lyre *(music)*, harp *(music)*, pipes *(music)* . . .

ASTROLOGER 2: and all kinds of music must fall down and worship the image of gold . . .

ASTROLOGER 1: and that whoever does not fall down and worship will be thrown into a blazing furnace.

ASTROLOGER 2: But there are some Jews whom you have set over the affairs of the province of Babylon—

ASTROLOGER 1: Shadrach, Meshach, and Abednego—

ASTROLOGER 2: Who pay no attention to you, O king.

ASTROLOGER 1: They neither serve your gods nor worship the image of gold you have set up.

NARRATOR 1: Furious with rage, Nebuchadnezzar summoned Shadrach, Meshach and Abednego.

NARRATOR 2: So these men were brought before the king,

NARRATOR 3: and Nebuchadnezzar said to them,

NEBUCHADNEZZAR: Is it true, Shadrach, Meshach and Abednego, that you do not serve my gods or worship the image of gold I have set up? Now when you hear the sound of the horn *(music)*, flute *(music)*, zither *(music)*, lyre *(music)*, harp *(music)*, pipes *(music)* and all kinds of music, if you are ready to fall down and worship the image I made, very good. But if you do not worship it, you will be thrown immediately into a blazing furnace. Then what god will be able to rescue you from my hand?

NARRATOR 3: Shadrach, Meshach and Abednego replied to the king.

SHADRACH: O Nebuchadnezzar, we need not defend ourselves before you in this matter.

MESHACH: If we are thrown into the blazing furnace, the God we serve is able to save us from it, and he will rescue us from your hand, O king.

ABEDNEGO: But even if he does not, we want you to know, O king, that we will not serve your gods or worship the image of gold you have set up.

NARRATOR 2: Then Nebuchadnezzar was furious with Shadrach, Meshach and Abednego, and his attitude toward them changed.

NARRATOR 3: He ordered the furnace heated seven times hotter than usual and commanded some of the strongest soldiers in his army to tie up Shadrach, Meshach and Abednego and throw them into the blazing furnace.

NARRATOR 2: The king's command was so urgent and the furnace so hot that the flames of the fire killed the men who took up Shadrach, Meshach and Abednego . . .

NARRATOR 3: and these three men, firmly tied, fell into the blazing furnace.

NARRATOR 1: Then King Nebuchadnezzar leaped to his feet in amazement and asked his advisers,

NEBUCHADNEZZAR: Wasn't it three men that we tied up and threw into the fire?

NARRATOR 2: They replied . . .

ASTROLOGERS 1 and 2: Certainly, O king.

NARRATOR 2: He said . . .

NEBUCHADNEZZAR: Look! I see four men walking around in the fire, unbound and unharmed, and the fourth looks like a son of the gods.

NARRATOR 3: Nebuchadnezzar then approached the opening of the blazing furnace and shouted.

NEBUCHADNEZZAR: Shadrach, Meshach and Abednego, servants of the Most High God, come out! Come here!

NARRATOR 1: So Shadrach, Meshach and Abednego came out of the fire, . . .

NARRATOR 2: and the satraps, prefects, governors, and royal advisers crowded around them.

NARRATOR 3: They saw that the fire had not harmed their bodies, nor was a hair on their heads singed;

NARRATOR 1: their robes were not scorched,

NARRATOR 2: and there was no smell of fire on them.

NARRATOR 3: Then Nebuchadnezzar said,

NEBUCHADNEZZAR: Praise be to the God of Shadrach, Meshach and Abednego, who has sent his angel and rescued his servants! They trusted in him and defied the king's command and were willing to give up their lives rather than serve or worship any god except their own God. Therefore, I decree that the people of any nation or language who say anything against the God of Shadrach, Meshach and Abednego be cut into pieces and their houses be turned into piles of rubble, for no other god can save in this way.

NARRATOR 1: Then the king promoted Shadrach, Meshach and Abednego in the province of Babylon.

ALL: Amen!

A Devotional Moment

Kodak moments are one thing, but devotional moments are something else. The Nebuchadnezzar script is fun to perform. When this writer uses it, I give a little brass desk bell to someone in the group to ring where the script suggests music. Because this passage is based on a Hebrew literary style, there is repetition and a rhythm of sorts. That's part of its charm. But the passage has more than charm, it has spiritual promise. What is that promise? Read Isaiah 43:2 in unison. This is one of the great promises of the Word. It relates to the so-called three Hebrew children.

Hosea:
A Love That Will Not Let Go

(A Monologue)

Scripture: Hosea 1

Theme: God's never-ending love

Cast: Hosea

Oh sure, I've been a preacher for most of my life. I can hardly remember when I wasn't. Successful? What do you mean by "successful"? I never made much money. And, frankly, the crowds never stopped to listen—that is until *she* came into my life. That's when everything changed. She? Oh, I think that's a story your readers would find interesting.

Like I said, I wasn't a major league preacher, you know, like the guys on television. No one ever heard of me, not at first anyway. I wasn't very happy by any stretch of the imagination. Of course, being a bachelor didn't help much. I remember so well, getting off the bus at the corner of my street and walking the half block to my house. I was weary and discouraged. There really wasn't much incentive to go home, but I couldn't afford to eat out. So, I'd go home after a day of exhorting and warm up a can of something in a saucepan.

Like I said, I wasn't very successful.

I used to stand on the corner across from the public library, where the taxi stand is, and warn the passersby about God's wrath—about how He was going to smite those hardened hearts and condemn to eternal punishment. I really worked over those folks who waited for the bus on Main at Third Avenue—from old man Gilbertson, the bank manager, to that red-headed paper boy who later got killed in Southeast Asia. Everybody was fair game for my message of hell fire.

The discouraging thing was that nobody listened to me. The tracts I pushed into their reluctant hands ended up on the sidewalk. I suspect the Almighty himself would have been rejected if He'd preached on that corner. I know what I preached was true. I believed it with all my heart. But people were not interested in hearing about the wrath to come. Frankly, as I look back on those days, I'm afraid my view of Father God was pretty much limited to the dark side of His nature. I just couldn't get very excited about a loving God—that is until Gomer entered my life.

Yeah, I know, I'm getting ahead of my story, but it's true. She made all the difference in the world. You just have to understand how unhappy and unsuccessful I was.

Well, on a particular warm Sunday evening, when I walked the half block to my house, I began to get an overpowering feeling that my luck was going to change. Yes, sir, when I scooped up *The Times* from the front yard, I distinctly heard a voice from somewhere say, "Happy days are almost here again!"

The house was stifling, so I left the front door open and pushed up a couple of windows. As I always did, I tossed my tract case onto a dining room chair and went out into the kitchen for a cold drink. The cold air from the fridge felt good on my face, but electric bills being what they are, I closed the door quickly and poured a glass of tea.

Sitting down at the table I glanced over the front page—that's when I spied a small story about a house of prostitution that had been raided. Accompanying the article was a photo of the vice squad officers herding the girls into a paddy wagon. A young woman in the foreground looked so forlorn that my heart went out to her. In the caption, she was quoted as saying, "I don't have the money to post bail, so I guess I'll have to spend the rest of my life in jail."

Like I said, I was smitten by that girl's picture and her words. Her face burned in my mind while my dinner boiled over on the stove. I studied the young woman's features and reread her admission, "I don't have the money." I can't say she was particularly attractive, but there was something about her face that spoke to my heart.

Then it was as if God in heaven spoke to me right there at my kitchen table. I could swear that I heard Him say, "I want you to go down to the Municipal Court Building and find this girl. She is part of my design for your life."

"A prostitute?" I said aloud to no one in particular. "What about my ministry? What will the neighbors say?"

All that night I sat up at my table. I was unable to shake the feeling that my life was in for a big change.

By morning I was reconciled to the idea of going down to the court building and finding her. After my usual cup of black coffee and bowl of cereal, I reached for my briefcase, then decided to leave it; to forget God's wrath for a few hours.

I'd never been inside the county building before, much less visit the lock-up area on the third floor.

Did I know why I was doing what I was doing? I don't think so. I must admit I had a romantic notion about the woman in that newspaper photo, but I think there was more to it than that; I had a distinct sense of oughtness. I knew that providence had something to do with my being there.

You better believe how nervous I was sitting there in the visitors room waiting to meet her. When the door opened a guard stuck his head in and asked, "Are you here to see Gomer?" I remember jumping to my feet and feeling my legs go to jelly, so I sat down. Then into the room walked a frightened young woman dressed in a shapeless gray dress.

It's funny, to this day I am unable to recall what we talked about in that forlorn room on that momentous morning. Also, I am unable to tell you when I first decided to take Gomer as my wife. But I did, and in time God gave us a daughter and two sons. Many a time on a warm summer evening when the kids were playing at the corner under the streetlight, and we sat on the front steps, I'd recall the face of that frightened woman who was feeling the wrath of society. Many times when I'd reach over and take her hand, she'd ask me to tell her one more time why I redeemed her. My answer was always the same, "Because I love you."

Did I continue preaching? Oh yes, but my message changed. It became so much easier to talk about God's love when you love and are loved.

Some Devotional Notes

The foregoing first person story may be presented as a read or memorized monologue. Or, you may wish to duplicate it and pass it out to be read as a meditation by the participants.

The following are additional devotional helps that you may use in conjunction with the monologue.

Duplicate this scripture paraphrase and arrangement, and use it as a group reading. It is based on the first chapter of Hosea.

ALL: When the Lord began to speak through Hosea, the Lord said to him,

MALE 1: Go, take to yourself a wife, an adulterous wife.

MALE 2: A wife, Lord? An adulterous wife? But why, Lord?

MALE 1: Because the land is guilty of the vilest adultery. The people have departed from the Lord.

MALE 2: But Lord . . .

MALE 1: Go to the harlots' house and find you a wife.

GROUP: So Hosea went, and he married Gomer [Go-mehr].

WOMEN: And she conceived and bore him a son.

FEMALE 1: See, Hosea, I have borne you a little boy.

GROUP: Then the Lord said to Hosea,

MALE 1: Call your son Jezreel, because I will put an end to the kingdom of Israel.

FEMALE 1: So be it, Hosea. His name shall be Jezreel.

WOMEN: Then Gomer conceived again and gave birth to a daughter.

FEMALE 1: See, my husband, I have borne you a little girl.

GROUP: Then the Lord said to Hosea,

MALE 1: Call your daughter Lo-Ruhamah, for I will no longer show love to the house of Israel. Yet I will show love to the house of Judah; and I will save them.

FEMALE 1: It shall be, Hosea. Her name shall be Lo-Ruhamah.

GROUP: After she had weaned Lo-Ruhamah, Gomer had another son.

MALE 1: You shall call this son Lo-Ammi, for you are not my people, and I am not your God.

GROUP: Yet the Israelites would become like the sand on the seashore, which cannot be counted.

MEN: In the place where it was said, "You are not my people," they will be called "sons of the living God.

WOMEN: The people of Judah and the people of Israel will be reunited."

MALE 1: Say of your brothers and sisters, "My loved one."

GROUP: Thanks be to God for Hosea's obedience.

- Improvise the conversation between the preacher and the woman when they first meet at the jail.
- Discuss and pray about unconditional love.
- Consider these words from the hymn "O Love That Will Not Let Me Go."

> *O Love, that will not let me go,*
> *I rest my weary soul in Thee.*
> *I give Thee back the life I owe,*
> *That in Thine ocean depths its flow*
> *May richer, fuller be.*
> —GEORGE MATHESON

Zaccheus: When Salvation Comes to Your House

Scripture: Luke 19:1-10

Theme: Discipleship

Cast: Interviewer, Zaccheus

Part 1

INTERVIEWER: So tell me, Mr. Z, now that you've moved out of your palatial mansion and into the small condo, how is the new lifestyle affecting you?

ZACCHEUS: Oh, I don't know, I got kinda lost wandering around in the old house. This place is pretty compact.

INTERVIEWER: I suppose that's one way of looking at it. But doesn't three rooms and a path leave something to be desired?

ZACCHEUS: Maybe on cold nights, but it's wonderful to be rid of all the excess baggage.

INTERVIEWER: Those Gobelin tapestries probably brought you a pretty penny at auction.

ZACCHEUS: That's not what I'm talking about, sir. The excess baggage I refer to was in my spirit.

INTERVIEWER: Ah ha, a conscience attack?

ZACCHEUS: Perhaps I need to set the record straight. Have a seat and let me tell you how I met my new Master.

Part 2

ZACCHEUS: Can I ever forget that morning—the morning of the day my whole world was turned upside down? When I awoke I had a sense of excitement, but I couldn't remember why this day was so important. I laid there in bed with the sheets pulled up to my chin, trying to shake sleep out of my head. I'm afraid I'd had one glass too many of that Spanish wine I'd imported.

There was no question, I should be excited about something, but what was it? My work was finally caught up and I'd filled out my latest report on my Jericho tax collections. Maybe that's why I was feeling so good . . .

Then it came crashing in, "Of course, today's the day Jesus of Nazareth is coming through Jericho!" The whole town was abuzz with excitement. Street vendors, pickpockets, and the police force alike were anticipating the occasion, though for different reasons.

I jumped up from bed. While my valet ran the bath water and selected my clothes for the day, I scanned the *Jericho Journal* for news about the Nazarene's itinerary. Buried in the religion page was a reported rumor surmising that Jesus was meeting friends at the third hour. Other than that, there was nothing else.

Glancing out the window, I estimated the hour. There was no time to check the garden sundial. After my bath and a quick breakfast (Cook always insisted I have breakfast; "Most important meal of the day," she'd say, "Maybe if you'd eaten better as a child, you'd have grown bigger!" I always meant to say something to her about her impertinence), I headed for town.

Believe it or not, crowds were gathering at the city gate and were beginning to line the boulevard. My curiosity began to boil. What was there about this itinerant preacher that caught the crowds' fancy? I'd heard other self-proclaimed preachers—even heard the baptist on a business trip to Jerusalem. Now, there was a fiery orator.

"Any idea when He's getting here?" a fruit vendor asked no one in particular.

"This morning's *Journal* estimated He'd arrive around the third hour," I volunteered.

The vendor peered at me through squinty eyes. "Say, aren't you Zacchaeus the tax collector?"

"That's right," I answered uneasily, hoping that no one else heard him. You see, my position in the community isn't exactly enviable. Truthfully, I am considered something just a notch or two above the Judean king who slaughtered all the boy babies 30 or so years ago. If you think I'm exaggerating, you should have heard what the good Jericho-ites hissed at me as they took other positions along the curb.

So, I just crossed over to the other side of the street to find a better vantage point. Every square inch of sidewalk was occupied by tall and hefty citizens who towered over me. Have I said it before? Some people consider me short, but I've always believed that size is in the mind. I've known a few men who could make Goliath nervous, who live and behave like dwarfs. Not so with me, I have prided myself in behavior that says you're in control of any situation. That's how I got assigned to this prosperous region. How do you think I got where I am, or maybe was.

From the town gate, and repeated down both sides of the street, buzzed the crowd, "Here he comes!" That's when the press started. All around me folks pushed forward, blocking my view of the Carpenter from Nazareth's entrance. The chant, "Here He comes . . . here He comes . . . here He comes" grew louder, and here I was in the back of the crowd. I looked up at the sycamore tree that stood right above me. A little boy had shimmied up and was seated on a limb that hung right over the street. "Hey there, boy," I called out. "You know it's against the law to climb these fig trees." His mother, standing right next to me, looked up and threatened,

"Ephraim, you get down here at once. Do you want to go to jail?"

"Ah, Ma," the boy whined, "all the boys climb these trees."

"Well, not you, young man."

When the boy came down and his mother dragged him away to find a better vantage point, I retraced his route up the trunk and then inched my way out along the overhanging bough. When a police officer came by, I tossed him down a coin or two, and he passed on by. When I got my balance and was able to lean forward to see where Jesus was, I was shocked to find that the young preacher was just a stone's throw away. I watched as He moved down the street in deep conversation with a couple of men I did not recognize. His followers worked the crowd, shaking hands and accepting small gifts of foodstuff.

And then the whole entourage came to a stop when Jesus paused, left His companions, and walked over to my tree. Every eye was on Him. Perched up there, I watched Him through my feet. He was right below me, and then He looked up. Every person in that crowd focused on yours truly. My heart stopped beating. I was caught in the intensity of His eyes. All of a sudden, we were alone together in that crowd.

"Zacchaeus." He spoke my name in a way I had never heard it said before. "Zacchaeus, come down, I am staying in your home today."

The people who heard Jesus' words were incredulous. "He's going to a tax collector's home?" they murmured. "Can you believe it?" Some were angry and responded with an ungracious, "Well, I never . . ."

I shimmied back down the tree trunk and came face-to-face with Jesus of Nazareth.

"Well, what are we waiting for?" He asked.

The crowd parted as Jesus and I walked down the sidewalk toward my neighborhood. Around us was a swirl of remarks, some of which caused the preacher to smile and look at me. It was as if He found it amusing to be accused of associating with a sinner.

I can't tell you what we talked about during our five- or six-block walk. My head was in a spin. A large crowd followed us. They were still agog over Jesus' interest in me. When we reached the gate to my home, Jesus paused as if taking it all in. My property was pretty impressive. I couldn't help but comment, "Oh, this is nothing, wait until you come inside." He had no comment.

The brief tour of my house from the front door to the banquet room should have impressed the prophet, who, it is said, has observed that He had no place to lay His head, but He said nothing. Even when I pointed out certain antique wall hangings and unusually fine pieces of furniture, He'd only nod. I served Him a fine spur-of-the-moment meal on museum-quality fine china, set on Damascus lace. Because I'd given my pantry butler the day off, I served the Nazarene myself, always pointing out quality and rarity.

Finally, when the dishes and table coverings were put away, Jesus, sitting across from me, asked the most pointed question I have ever heard, "Zacchaeus, do you realize that today the Son of Man has come to your house, to seek and to save what was lost?"

The way He spoke that simple question caused a floodgate of emotion and sorrow to open within me. I suddenly realized that I was on my knees crying and praying. All of my dishonesty and hatred overwhelmed me. The hundreds I had cheated were like a jury, condemning me to death. And then I heard myself speak,

"Look, Lord! Here and now I promise to give half of my possessions to the poor. And I will pay back four times the amount I have swindled anyone out of."

When I had finished wrestling with my conscience and confessing my need to be forgiven, I stood and went to the balcony, under which the crowds from town stood. To them I repeated what I had promised God. A shout went up, and for the first time in all my adult life, I heard people praising the name of Zacchaeus.

Jesus stood next to me and said, "Today salvation has come to your house."

Part 3

ZACCHAEUS: So that, young man, is my story.

INTERVIEWER: But don't you miss all of your possessions?

ZACCHAEUS: As the Master says, what good would it be if I still had all those things, but lost my soul?

Some Devotional Exercises

● Compose a letter that Zacchaeus might have written to one of the Jericho citizens he cheated. Share it with the rest of the group as a monologue.

● Mime Zacchaeus and the sycamore tree incident.

● Make a list of those things or those people who tend to make you think more about yourself than others, or make you feel superior to other people. Talk to God about these influences.

Script and/or Scripture arrangement from *Acts of Worship*, by Wyatt and Miller, © 1995. Lillenas Publishing House. All rights reserved. Scripture quotes and paraphrases are from the *Holy Bible, New International Version*® (NIV®). Copyright © 1973, 1978, 1984 by International Bible Society. Used by permission of Zondervan Publishing House. All rights reserved.

Peter and John: What I Have I Give to You

Scripture: Acts 3—4

Theme: We each have something to share with others.

Cast: Leader, Men, Women, Man, Peter, Group

LEADER: It was the resurrected Jesus who said, "You will receive power when the Holy Spirit comes on you; and you will be my witnesses." Our worship time is based on the Acts of the Apostles, but it will concern itself with the Acts of Disciples—20th-century followers who use voice and movement and spirit to worship. Come, let us worship.

[You may sing or have a moment of silent prayer.]

LEADER: On those pages that record the Acts of the Apostles, it is written; one day Peter and John were going up to the temple at the time of prayer—at three in the afternoon.

MEN: Now a man crippled from birth was being carried to the temple gate called Beautiful.

WOMEN: This is where he was put every day to beg from those going into the temple courts.

LEADER: When the lame man saw Peter and John about to enter, he asked,

MAN: Sirs, do you have a gift for me?

LEADER: Peter looked straight at him and said,

PETER: Silver or gold I do not have, but what I have I give you.

MAN: And what is that?

PETER: In the name of Jesus Christ of Nazareth, walk!

MEN: Taking him by the right hand, Peter helped him up.

MAN: Be careful. I have not been able to . . .

ALL: And instantly the man's feet and ankles became strong.

MAN: I walk! I walk! I walk!

WOMEN: With great excitement, the man went with Peter and John into the temple courts . . .

46

MEN: Walking and jumping . . .

ALL: And praising God!

[You may pause here and discuss PETER's *words, "What I have I give you." What are we giving?]*

LEADER: Because of Peter's witness and the lame man's healing, a great group of people became believers, and the church in Jerusalem swelled to 5,000.

MEN: But then, because of the furor caused by the healing,

WOMEN: Peter and James were brought before the Sanhedrin.

LEADER: At once, the Sanhedrin realized that Peter and John were ordinary men, but it was obvious they had been with Jesus.

MEN: In their anger the Sanhedrin demanded,

ALL: By what power or what name did you do this thing to this lame man?

LEADER: Then Peter, filled with the Holy Spirit, said to them,

PETER: It is by the name of Jesus Christ of Nazareth, whom you crucified but whom God raised from the dead, that this man stands before you healed.

MEN: Jesus is the stone you builders rejected,

WOMEN: Which has become the capstone.

PETER: Salvation is found in no one else,

ALL: For there is no other name under heaven given to us by which we must be saved.

LEADER: Then the Sanhedrin leaders called Peter and John and shouted,

ALL: We command you; speak no more in that name!

MEN: What name?

ALL: His name!

WOMEN: Whose name?

ALL: In the name of Jesus!

PETER: But we cannot help speaking about what we have seen and heard.

ALL: Then all of the people praised the Lord.

[An affirmation: God grant that all with whom I come in contact (today, tomorrow) will know that I have been with Jesus. Amen.]

Stephen: Making a Difference

Scripture: Acts 6—7

Theme: Wanted—people whose presence make a difference in their several worlds

Cast: Leader, Men, Women, Person 1, Person 2, Person 3, Stephen, All

---

LEADER: From an unknown disciple comes the comforting concept that we are surrounded by a "great cloud of witnesses." The Acts of the Apostles is a record of many of those witnesses—not the least of whom was Stephen, a man full of faith, grace, power, and the Holy Spirit. During this worship time, we will turn to the source of faith, grace, and power—the Spirit of God.

[You may sing or have a moment of silent prayer.]

LEADER: This is a story that begins in Jerusalem in the days when the number of disciples was increasing.

WOMEN: When Grecian Jewish women complained because they were being overlooked . . .

MEN: the Twelve gathered all the disciples together and said,

ALL: Choose seven men who are full of the Spirit and wise.

PERSON 1: So, who shall we select?

PERSON 2: I say they should be Greek.

PERSON 3: Then I nominate Nicanor.

PERSON 2: And I select both Timon and Parmenas.

PERSON 1: Don't forget Nicolas from Antioch.

PERSON 3: And I nominate Stephen. We all know him to be a man full of . . .

MEN: faith!

PERSON 1: And full of . . .

WOMEN: grace!

PERSON 2: And I have found him to be a man filled with . . .

48

ALL: power and the Holy Spirit!

[You may pause here and discuss the three qualities—faith, grace, and power—and how they relate to a drama ministry.]

LEADER: Stephen's Greek name means "crown." Tradition tells us that his father was Gentile and his mother, Jewish. Because his family may have been wealthy, he was raised in the Hellenistic (or Greek) tradition. Some believe Stephen was present in the Upper Room on Pentecost. He was a young leader, who, like Peter and John, could not help but speak about all he had seen and heard.

PERSON 1: Stephen! Stop speaking about your Jesus.

PERSON 2: Stephen! If you do not stop speaking, we will silence you!

PERSON 3: Stephen, stop! You are blaspheming Moses!

PERSON 2: Stephen, stop! We don't want your Christ!

PERSON 1: Stephen, stop!

LEADER: When Stephen would not be silenced, they took him to trial.

PERSON 3: I heard him say that his dead Jesus . . .

PERSON 1: I heard him say that his dead Jesus will . . .

PERSON 2: I heard him say that Jesus is Messiah!

LEADER: Stephen stood among his accusers, when suddenly one called out . . .

PERSON 3: Look, his face is shining like the face of an angel!

ALL: He is shining like an angel.

PERSON 1: Are these charges true?

LEADER: There was a long silence. Then Stephen stood and replied,

STEPHEN: Do not resist the Holy Spirit.

LEADER: Then Stephen, full of the Holy Spirit, looked up to heaven . . .

PERSON 2: See his face? He has the glow of heaven upon him.

PERSON: Listen, he's saying something.

STEPHEN: Look, I see heaven open, and the Son of Man is standing at the right hand of God.

LEADER: When the Sanhedrin heard these words, they were furious. They gnashed their teeth and yelled at the top of their voices . . .

ALL: Blasphemer! . . . Away with this man! . . . Stone him to death!

MEN: Stone him!

WOMEN: Yes, stone him!

LEADER: So frightened and desperate men dragged Stephen out beyond the city walls to put him to death. They picked up stones left from other executions; judged their weight and estimated what damage they could do to the young man who was filled with God's Spirit.

PERSON 1: Look at the arrowhead point on this stone . . .

PERSON 3: And heft the weight of this one.

LEADER: Then the cowardly crowd removed their coats and threw them at the feet of one Saul, a religious leader from Tarsus.

PERSON 1: Take this, Stephen!

PERSON 2: And this!

PERSON 3: This will shut his profane mouth.

PERSON 2 and 3: Kill him!

PERSON 1: Silence the blasphemer!

LEADER: The bleeding Stephen pulled himself up, and tried to stand, but he fell to his knees.

PERSON 3: Listen, he's going to speak.

STEPHEN: Lord, do not hold this sin against them.

ALL: Father, forgive them, for they do not know what they are doing.

STEPHEN: Lord Jesus, receive my spirit.

ALL: Father, into your hands I give my spirit.

LEADER: With that, Stephen, a man full of faith, grace, power, and the Holy Spirit, surrendered his life.

ALL: He who loses his life for my sake will find it.

LEADER: A transfixed Saul witnessed the execution, and in his silence gave approval to Stephen's death.

PERSON 1: Saul. Saul of Tarsus, are you going to let the rest of the blasphemers go free?

LEADER: The Word describes Saul's rage toward the Christian community. On the very day of Stephen's murder, a great persecution broke out; Saul was determined to destroy the church. No one was safe from the sword, until one day on a road to Damascus, Saul the destroyer became Paul the believer.

PERSON 1: Imprinted upon his mind and heart was the memory of a man full of . . .

ALL: faith, grace, power, and the Holy Spirit.

STEPHEN: A young man whose presence made a difference.

An affirmation: *God grant that in my several worlds, my faith, God's grace, and the power of the Holy Spirit shall be felt through me.*

Considering Stephen

The concept that Stephen was a young man who was "full of faith, grace, power, and God's Holy Spirit" is important to this passage. The participants in this devotional should be given an opportunity to analyze "faith," "grace," and "power," as it relates to those with a sense of ministry.

- Improvise ways of describing faith: both what it is and what it isn't.
- Do the same for grace. This writer has often felt that grace is the quality of life that bespeaks Christ in your life, even when you don't open your mouth.
- Finally, consider power in the light of Acts 6:8, "Stephen, a man full of God's grace and power, did great wonders and miraculous signs among the people."
- Improv a conversation between Stephen and Paul regarding the young man's influence on the great apostle.

Paul and Timothy: Be Prepared

Scripture: 2 Timothy 4: 1-18

Theme: Preparation for ministry

Cast: Paul, Timothy, Luke, Group

Dramatic Interlude 1

PAUL: And you, young man, what is your name?

TIMOTHY: Timothy, sir.

PAUL: Are you a believer?

TIMOTHY: A believer, sir?

PAUL: Yes, a believer in Jesus the Christ. Does His Spirit live in you?

TIMOTHY: Oh yes, sir. I became a Christian when you were preaching in Lystra. Since then, I have been taught the things of God by my mother and grandmother.

PAUL: Say, they wouldn't be Lois and Eunice, now, would they?

TIMOTHY: That's exactly who they are. Do you remember them from Lystra?

PAUL: Indeed I do. And I have also learned of your commitment and influence. For a young man, you have a great deal of maturity in the things of God.

TIMOTHY: My greatest goal is to preach Jesus Christ.

PAUL: Then tell me, Timothy, would you be willing to join me in ministry?

TIMOTHY: You mean leave Lystra?

PAUL: Not only leave Lystra, but take Christ's gospel to the far-flung corners of our world.

TIMOTHY: And I would be your traveling companion?

PAUL: That's right. John Mark has left us, so Silas and I need help. I think you're the one to provide it. What do you say?

TIMOTHY *(hesitantly):* Before I say yes, would you tell me something?

PAUL: Of course, anything.

TIMOTHY: Why did John Mark decide to leave the ministry?

PAUL *(with a note of sadness):* That's a fair question, young man. First of all, understand, I believe John Mark to be a worthy minister. However, I believe he is no longer with me because of a disagreement in which I became impatient and boorish. I am quick to add that I've learned a lesson or two from that experience, as well as from my dear old friend Barnabas. He was quick to point out that patience is a fruit of living in Christ.

TIMOTHY: Well then, what can I say but, yes, I'll join you and Silas. *(Pause)* There's one thing more, Paul.

PAUL: What's that?

TIMOTHY: In school I was taught, in a job interview, to ask the senior pastor what his concept of ministry is. So, what is ministry to you?

PAUL *(warmly):* Hmmmm, I've wrestled with that question for many years, Timothy. I still remember the event that helped turn my life around and that eventually came into play in formulating my concept of ministry.

TIMOTHY: Are you referring to Stephen's martyrdom?

PAUL: Exactly. What I saw in a man that day made such a deep impression that I tried to tear it from my mind's eye by doing great harm to all Christians everywhere. But the memory of that young minister followed me, until I came face-to-face with Jesus the Christ on a highway into Damascus. That's when I made another discovery about ministry, this time from the hands of one Ananias of Damascus. From him and other believers I learned the secret of ministry. It may wear different cloaks, but its common denominator is to love people and see them through the eyes of Christ Jesus. That's what I expect from you, Timothy.

Optional Scripture Reading
2 Timothy 4:1-5

LEADER: In the presence of God and of Christ Jesus . . . I give you this:

GROUP: Preach the Word,

WOMAN: be prepared in season and out of season;

MEN: correct,

WOMAN: rebuke and encourage—

GROUP: with great patience and careful instruction.

LEADER: Keep your head in all situations,

MEN: endure hardships,

WOMAN: do the work of an evangelist,

GROUP: discharge all the duties of your ministry.

Dramatic Interlude 2

LUKE: I'm a physician, guard. Please let me see my patient.

PAUL: Is that you, Luke?

LUKE: It's me, Paul. So, you're still writing?

PAUL: Yes, it's a postscript on my letter to Timothy—to my "son."

LUKE: You've been at this one for a long while, Paul.

PAUL: I know, and I'm savoring every minute of it. As I write I keep recalling the day Timothy asked me about my concept of ministry. I think he knows, don't you? Listen to these words as if you were Timothy: "I give you this charge: Proclaim the Word; be prepared in season and out of season; correct, rebuke and encourage—with great patience and careful instruction. Timothy, keep your head in all situations, endure hardship, do the work of an evangelist, continue to discharge all the duties of your ministry." That's what it's all about, isn't it, Doc?

LUKE: So, old man, are you ready for your last journey?

PAUL: If you mean by foot or creaking vessel, the answer is no. *(Warmly)* But if you mean my final journey that will take me to the One whose prisoner I am, the answer is yes.

LUKE: When will you see Timothy again, Paul?

PAUL: I really don't know, on this side. Perhaps I need to ask him to come quickly. Winter is almost upon us. I'm not sure if I can take this leaking, rat-infested cistern much longer without my coat and some books.

LUKE: What can I do, Paul?

PAUL *(distracted):* Hmmm?

LUKE: I'd like to make your days a little more comfortable, old friend, if I can.

PAUL: Thank you, Luke. You well care for my body. I have the Father for my soul. Now I need Timothy for my spirit. I do hope he can get here before winter.

Optional Scripture Reading

LEADER: The apostle Paul continues: I am already being poured out like a drink offering, and the time has come for my departure.

MEN: I have fought the good fight,

LEADER: I have finished the race,

WOMEN: I have kept the faith.

GROUP: Now there is in store for me a crown of righteousness,

LEADER: Which the Lord, the righteous Judge, will award on that day—

GROUP: Not only to me, but also to all who have longed for his appearing.

Improving on This Passage

The second dramatic interlude above deals with an older man who has come to the end of his ministry. When one reads the fourth chapter of 2 Timothy, one discovers a note of wistfulness and finality; human emotions of a servant who has run his course and sees the prize just out ahead.

Those who have visited the traditional site of Paul's final imprisonment in Rome, the subterranean Mammertine Prison, across the road from the Forum, can imagine the apostle's discomfort and dread of a Roman winter. No place in all of his writings does Paul show his vulnerability to the degree that he does in these closing verses of 2 Timothy.

Now, spend some time with these exercises. They will stretch your imagination and your heart.

- Improvise Paul's defense of his God who allowed this imprisonment, to his prison guard.
- It probably could not happen, but turn your imagination loose on a monologue letter from Timothy's mother Eunice to Paul.
- Work on a conversation between Timothy's mother and Grandmother Lois, about their son's and grandson's ministry with Paul.
- In mime, reenact the apostle's plea to Timothy, about coming before winter, and what to bring.

Acts of Worship:

Elements of the Dramatic

While our purpose is ministry, the elements of drama remain steadfast. Regardless of Christian or so-called secular purposes, those qualities must be present in sketches, one-acts, or full-length plays; in other words, these are what make a script and production dramatic: creativity, imagination, dialogue, characterization, as well as the technical stuff like auditions, lighting, makeup, and the rest.

Many of these theatre elements have spiritual implications that you and your group ought to pursue. That's the thrust of this section. Spend a few moments with the participants of your meeting or rehearsal and focus on things of the spirit, as they relate to the your specific ministry—drama.

Lillenas Drama

Creator, Creation, Creativity

Scripture: Genesis 1:1-3, 26-27, 31; Psalm 8

Theme: Human creativity begins and ends with the Creator who created us.

Cast: Leader, Reader 1, Reader 2, Group

LEADER: O LORD!

GROUP: Our Lord!

LEADER: How majestic is your name . . .

GROUP: in all the earth!

LEADER: With the psalmist, let us celebrate the Creator of the heavens and the earth.

GROUP: Our Creator!

READER 1: In the beginning God created . . .

LEADER: In the beginning God created the heavens and the earth. In the beginning God brought order out of disorder.

READER 1: Now the earth was formless and empty; darkness was over the surface of the deep,

READER 2: and the Spirit of God was hovering over the waters.

LEADER: Even in the midst of a major metropolis, the gray sameness cannot contain the beauty of God's creation forever. Even the tallest monument to human ingenuity cannot completely obscure a dazzling sunset.

READER 1: And God said, "Let there be light,"

READER 2: and there was light.

LEADER: Even the multihued light of sunset. Sunsets of layered purple and red and orange energized then captured by the fading light. Sunsets of wispy clouds flecked with gold wandering the horizon.

In the wild intensity of a sunset is revealed the depth of God's creativity. While God creates intentionally ("God said") and God's creation is orderly ("it was good"), still God creates with a freedom that is reflected in all of creation. Creation does not stand still and will not be stilled. Seething with unbounded energy, all of creation sings the praises of the Creator. The psalmist knew this.

READER 1: O LORD, when I consider . . .

READER 2: O LORD when I consider your heavens,

READER 1: O LORD when I consider the work of your fingers,

READER 2: O LORD when I consider the moon and the stars, which you have set in place,

READER 1: O LORD when I consider . . .

READER 2: What is man that you are mindful of him,

READER 1: O LORD when I consider . . .

READER 2: What is the son of man that you care for him?

LEADER: Then God said, "Let us make man in our image, in our likeness."

READER 1: So God created man in his own image, in the image of God he created him;

READER 2: male and female he created them.

LEADER: God is the inspiration for human creativity. So, we create with purpose and order, but the wildness and freedom celebrated by sunsets may also be found in human creativity. Our creativity is involved in every aspect of drama ministry, and our use of creativity in ministry glorifies the God who created us.

READER 1: O LORD, you made us a little lower than the heavenly beings.

READER 2: O LORD, you crowned us with glory and honor.

LEADER: God saw all that he had made, and it was very good.

GROUP: To God be the glory.

LEADER: Let us pray.
Father, You have created us and have
put us on this earth for a purpose.
You have sent Your Son to die for us and
You are calling us to complete Your work.
By Your hand Christ has been raised and is exalted.
And You give us hope to continue the work of Christ.
Now send Your Holy Spirit to help us to be
the ministers You have called us to become.

GROUP: Amen.

The Power of Images

Scripture: 1 Timothy: 6:15-16; Exodus 33:20-23; Genesis 1:28; Psalm 139:1, 13-14; John 1:1, 14, 18; 1 John 3:2

Theme: Imagination is God's gift, not a replacement for God.

Cast: Leader, Reader 1, Reader 2, Group

LEADER: God, the blessed and only Ruler, the King of kings and Lord of lords, who alone is immortal and who lives in unapproachable light, whom no one has seen or can see.

GROUP: To God be honor and might forever.

LEADER: "Whom no one has seen or can see."

READER 1: And the LORD said to Moses, "I will do everything you have asked, because I am pleased with you and I know you by name."

READER 2: Then Moses said, "Now show me your glory."

READER 1: And the LORD said, "I will cause all my goodness to pass in front of you, and I will proclaim my name, the LORD, in your presence. I will have mercy on whom I will have mercy, and I will have compassion on whom I will have compassion."

READER 2: "But," [God] said, "you cannot see my face, for no one may see me and live."

LEADER: Since we are not able to see God (and live), we create mental images to describe our experiences of God. Often God is described in Scripture as possessing human emotions and characteristics. This type of pictorial language is employed later in this same passage when Moses boldly requests to see God.

READER 1: Then the LORD said, "There is a place near me where you may stand on a rock. When my glory passes by, I will put you in a cleft in the rock and cover you with my hand until I have passed by. Then I will remove my hand and you will see my back;"

READER 2: "but my face must not be seen."

LEADER: One of the most beautiful images of God is evoked by the psalmist.

READER 1: [God] will cover you with his feathers,

READER 2: And under his wings you will find refuge;

LEADER: Of course we are not to take this image of God literally as a hen caring for her brood. The image is intended to describe the psalmist's experience of God's love and faithfulness.

God uses these powerful images to reveal himself, but with them comes the warning that the images are no substitute for God. The warning is clear in the commandment prohibiting graven images. The second commandment reads: "You shall not make for yourself an idol in the form of anything in heaven above or on the earth beneath or in the waters below" (Exodus 20:4).

We, like Israel, must understand the danger of abusing our God-given imagination. Because we are created in God's image, our image of who God is can and does profoundly affect our perception of ourselves, of others, and of our world.

READER 1: Then God said, "Let us make man in our image, in our likeness."

READER 2: So God created man in his own image, in the image of God he created him;

GROUP: male and female he created them.

LEADER: O LORD, you have searched me.

GROUP: O LORD, you know us.

READER 1: For you created my inmost being; you knit me together in my mother's womb.

READER 2: I praise you because I am fearfully and wonderfully made;

GROUP: O LORD, your works are wonderful!

LEADER: For Christians, the use of our imagination demands even more attention and care because of our confession that God has created in Jesus Christ the perfect image of himself in human form. As Paul writes in Colossians, Christ "is the image of the invisible God, the firstborn over all creation" (1:15), and again to the Christians at Corinth: "The god of this age has blinded the minds of unbelievers, so that they cannot see the light of the gospel of the glory of Christ, who is the image of God" (2 Corinthians 4:4).

READER 1: In the beginning was the Word, and the Word was with God,

GROUP: and the Word was God.

READER 2: He was with God in the beginning.

READER 1: The Word became flesh and made his dwelling among us.

GROUP: We have seen his glory,

READER 2: the glory of the Only Begotten, who came from the Father,

GROUP: full of grace and truth.

READER 1: No one has ever seen God,

READER 2: but the only begotten Son, who is at the Father's side, has made him known.

LEADER: Because of the importance and power of images we must commit ourselves to the careful use of our imagination. We must not force religious imagination to exist only on the creative fringe. Neither can we indiscriminately borrow the disposable images generated by our consumer society.

We must continually subject our imagination to self-examination. Can we create images without turning them into idols? We must take the risk. Avoiding religious imagination does not glorify the God who Christ imaged and who imagines what we may become.

READER 1: In 2 Corinthians, Paul writes: "And we, who with unveiled faces all reflect the Lord's glory, are being transformed into his likeness with ever-increasing glory, which comes from the Lord, who is the Spirit" (3:18).

READER 2: And in Colossians: "Do not lie to each other, since you have taken off your old self with its practices and have put on the new self, which is being renewed in knowledge in the image of its Creator" (3:10).

READER 1: Dear friends, now we are children of God,

READER 2: and what we will be has not yet been made known.

LEADER: But we know that when he appears, we shall be like him,

GROUP: for we shall see him as he is.

Imagination and the Community

Scripture: Psalm 131; Matthew 18:1-4; 1 Corinthians 13:1-8*a*

Theme: Imagination is a gift that must be shared with others.

Cast: Leader, Reader 1, Reader 2, Group, All

LEADER: My heart is not proud, O LORD, my eyes are not haughty;

GROUP: Our hope is in the LORD.

LEADER: I do not concern myself with great matters or things too wonderful for me.

GROUP: Our hope is in the LORD!

LEADER: But I have stilled my soul;

GROUP: like a weaned child with its mother;

LEADER: and I have quieted my soul;

GROUP: like a weaned child is my soul within me.

LEADER: Put your hope in the LORD.

GROUP: We will both now and forevermore.

READER 1: At that time the disciples came to Jesus and asked, "Who is the greatest in the kingdom of heaven?"

READER 2: He called a little child and had him stand among them. And he said: "I tell you the truth, unless you change and become like little children, you will never enter the kingdom of heaven. Therefore, whoever humbles himself like this child is the greatest in the kingdom of heaven."

LEADER: We too easily succumb to "who is the greatest" thinking. We are guilty of it when we decide who is the best or who is more important. Who is the best actor? Who is more important—the performers or the technical staff?

"Who is the greatest" thinking is self-defeating. Everyone is important to the production and each contributes imagination in completing the assigned task. This thinking restricts our imagination because we are more concerned about comparing our contribution with that of someone else.

Instead we ought to approach our work with the wide-eyed sense of wonder we see in children. Without "who is the greatest" concerns, our imagination is free to wonder, to see the extraordinary in the ordinary, to discover order where there only seems to be disorder. This is the characteristic of imagination that needs to be a part of every aspect of the production.

The purpose of imagination is not to call attention to ourselves but to call the audience to participate—to exercise their own imaginations. Imagination is one way that we experience God's presence. Sharing our imagination with each other helps us to come together in worship and experience God's presence in the community. As we make public our private images of God and the world, we learn from each other. When we allow each other to appreciate and enjoy our private images, we enhance our communion with God and with each other.

Without the participation of the audience in the imagination process any performance, no matter how well it is done, is little better than a noisy gong or a clanging cymbal.

LEADER: And now I will show you the most excellent way.

READER 1: If I speak in the tongues of men and of angels, but have not love,

READER 2: I am only a resounding gong or a clanging cymbal.

READER 1: If I have the gift of prophecy and can fathom all mysteries and all knowledge, and if I have a faith that can move mountains, but have not love,

READER 2: I am nothing.

READER 1: If I give all I possess to the poor and surrender my body to the flames, but have not love,

READER 2: I gain nothing.

LEADER: Love is patient, love is kind.

GROUP: [Love] does not envy,

LEADER: [Love] does not boast,

GROUP: [Love] is not proud.

READER 1: [Love] is not rude, it is not self-seeking,

READER 2: [Love] is not easily angered, it keeps no record of wrongs.

READER 1: Love does not delight in evil but rejoices with the truth.

READER 2: [Love] always protects, always trusts, always hopes, always perseveres.

ALL: Love never fails.

Observation Is the Key to Character

Scripture: Hebrews 1:1-3; 11; 12:1-3

Theme: Character is developed through observing and imitating others. Christian character comes from observing Christ and participating in His suffering.

Cast: Leader, Group

LEADER: In the past God spoke to our forefathers through the prophets at many times and in various ways,

GROUP: but in these last days he has spoken to us by his Son,

LEADER: whom he appointed heir of all things,

GROUP: and through whom he made the universe.

LEADER: The Son is the radiance of God's glory and the exact representation of his being,

GROUP: sustaining all things by his powerful word.

[Let everyone take a turn reading the following "by faiths."]

By faith Abel offered God a better sacrifice than Cain did.

By faith Noah, when warned about things not yet seen, in holy fear built an ark to save his family.

By faith Abraham, when called to go to a place he would later receive as his inheritance, obeyed and went, even though he did not know where he was going.

By faith Isaac blessed Jacob and Esau in regard to their future.

By faith Jacob, when he was dying, blessed each of Joseph's sons and worshiped as he leaned on the top of his staff.

By faith Joseph, when his end was near, spoke about the exodus of the Israelites from Egypt and gave instructions about his bones.

By faith Moses' parents hid him for three months after he was born, because they saw he was no ordinary child, and they were not afraid of the king's edict.

By faith the people passed through the Red Sea.

By faith the walls of Jericho fell.

By faith the prostitute Rahab, because she welcomed the spies, was not killed.

LEADER: And what more shall I say? I do not have time to tell about Gideon, Barak, Samson, Jephthah, David, Samuel and the prophets, who through faith conquered kingdoms, administered justice, and gained what was promised; who shut the mouths of lions, quenched the fury of flames, and escaped the edge of the sword; whose weakness was turned to strength; and who became powerful in battle and routed foreign armies.

GROUP: The world was not worthy of them.

LEADER: Others were tortured and refused to be released, so that they might gain a better resurrection.

GROUP: The world was not worthy of them.

LEADER: Some faced jeers and flogging, while still others were chained and put in prison.

GROUP: The world was not worthy of them.

LEADER: They were stoned; the were sawed in two; they were put to death by the sword.

GROUP: The world was not worthy of them.

LEADER: They went about in sheepskins and goatskins, destitute, persecuted and mistreated—

GROUP: The world was not worthy of them.

LEADER: Therefore, since we are surrounded by such a great cloud of witnesses, let us throw off everything that hinders and the sin that so easily entangles,

GROUP: and let us run with perseverance the race marked out for us.

LEADER: One of the best tools an actor has to develop a character is observation. Observation of clues from the other characters in a script and from the script itself, will help an actor discover the qualities or features that set apart the character they are portraying from the rest of the cast. Observation is also important to giving life to a character on the stage. Observation allows the actor to discover the "talk" or the "walk" that defines the character being portrayed.

Observation is also important off the stage. It started soon after we came into this world. We watched the weird things our parents did and tried to imitate them. From them and from others who contributed to our lives, we have developed the character that defines who we are, that sets us apart from everyone else.

In the famous "hall of faith" passage we read together, the author of Hebrews is lifting up examples of outstanding faith for us to observe and to imitate. These great examples of faith will be important to our Christian character. Of course, if we truly hope to be like Christ we will eventually need to come and observe Christ. Observe Christ today in Scripture—in the Old Testament, in the Gospels, in the Epistles to early Christians. Observe Christ in other people. Above all, let other people observe Christ in you.

LEADER: Let us fix our eyes on Jesus,

GROUP: the author and perfecter of our faith,

LEADER: who for the joy set before him endured the cross, scorning its shame,

GROUP: and sat down at the right hand of the throne of God.

LEADER: Consider him who endured such opposition from sinful men, so that you will not grow weary and lose heart.

Be Actors, Not Hypocrites

Scripture: Matthew 6:5; 7:1-5, 12; Psalm 25:1-7

Theme: Integrity is crucial to an effective drama ministry.

Cast: Leader, Reader 1, Reader 2, Group

LEADER: To you, O LORD, I lift up my soul;

GROUP: In you I trust, O my God.

READER 1: And when you pray, do not be like the hypocrites,

READER 2: They love to pray standing in the synagogues and on the street corners to be seen by men.

LEADER: Have you ever been accused of being an "actor"? "You actors," Jesus said to the crowd, "you care nothing for God in your prayers but only yourselves."

Jesus was not the first to underscore the shortcomings of the Greek theatre. Many of Greece's own philosophers had for many years viewed the stage as a sham and accused the actors of being merely deceivers.

The actors performing in the arenas around Jerusalem were generally more interested in calling attention to themselves. These actors cared little about the character they portrayed or the stories they reenacted.

Jesus had more to say to the crowd . . .

READER 1: Do not judge, or you too will be judged.

READER 2: For in the same way you judge others, you will be judged, and with the measure you use, it will be measured to you.

READER 1: Why do you look at the speck of sawdust in your brother's eye and pay no attention to the plank in your own eye?

READER 2: How can you say to your brother, "Let me take the speck out of your eye," when all the time there is a plank in your own eye?

READER 1: You hypocrite, first take the plank out of your own eye, and then you will see clearly to remove the speck from your brother's eye.

READER 2: So in everything, do to others what you would have them do to you, for this sums up the Law and the Prophets.

LEADER: Again Jesus accuses the crowd of being "actors."

Jesus was calling the crowd to live with itegrity among themselves.

The call was, and still is, to live a life of love for God and for each other and not merely to pretend to live that live.

It is easy to find fault with others while covering up our own short-comings. The one who does this is hiding behind a mask and cannot be a truly genuine or transparent person. So, when Jesus called the crowd "actors" He was not referring specifically to the profession of acting, but to the masks that were commonly worn by actors of that day. The actor's mask had come to be associated with deception and symbolized how far the actors had fallen from the integrity that had once characterized Greek drama.

Is our drama ministry characterized by integrity? Is it truly in the service of the Kingdom, or is it merely pretending to be? Does our drama group remember the importance of the story it is seeking to retell in each performance? That is the story of God's love. Pursue peace and be merciful as you tell the story. And if you are an actor, then be an actor with integrity and not a "hypocrite." That would probably include the backstage crew and everyone else.

READER 1: [O LORD] no one whose hope is in you will ever be put to shame,

READER 2: But they will be put to shame who are treacherous without excuse.

LEADER: Show me your ways, O LORD,

GROUP: teach me your paths;

LEADER: guide me in your truth and teach me, for you are God my Savior,

GROUP: and my hope is in you all day long.

LEADER: Remember, O LORD, your great mercy and love,

GROUP: for they are from of old,

LEADER: remember not the sins of my youth and my rebellious ways; according to your love remember me,

GROUP: for you are good, O LORD.

Script and/or Scripture arrangement from *Acts of Worship*, by Wyatt and Miller, © 1995. Lillenas Publishing House. All rights reserved. Scripture quotes and paraphrases are from the *Holy Bible, New International Version*® (NIV®). Copyright © 1973, 1978, 1984 by International Bible Society. Used by permission of Zondervan Publishing House. All rights reserved.

Light That Shines on Everyone

Scripture: Isaiah 2:5; John 1:4-9; Ephesians 5:8-14; Psalm 36:5-9

Theme: Christ comes to us as a Light in the darkness. We must decide to walk in the light or remain in the darkness. The choice is ours.

Cast: Leader, Reader 1, Reader 2, Group

LEADER: Come, let us walk in the light of the LORD.

READER 1: In him was life, and that life was the light of men. The light shines in the darkness, but the darkness has not understood.

READER 2: There came a man who was sent from God; his name was John.

READER 1: He came as a witness to testify concerning that light, so that through him all men might believe.

GROUP: He himself was not the light;

READER 1: He came only as a witness to the light.

READER 2: The true light that gives light to every man was coming into the world.

LEADER: Your love, O LORD, reaches to the heavens, your faithfulness to the skies.

GROUP: How priceless is your unfailing love!

LEADER: Your righteousness is like the mighty mountains, your justice like the great deep.

GROUP: How priceless is your unfailing love!

LEADER: O LORD, you preserve both man and beast.

GROUP: How priceless is your unfailing love!

LEADER: Both high and low among men find refuge in the shadow of your wings.

GROUP: For with you is the fountain of life;

LEADER: they feast on the abundance of your house; you give them drink from your river of delights.

GROUP: In your light we see light.

Identify the characters in John 9:1-41, the story of the man who was born blind, and assign someone to each part. Read the story together and then discuss the importance of light in the story. How does light and *the* Light (see John 1:5; 8:12) affect each of the characters in the story?

Acts of Worship:

The Covenant Group

The goal of drama as ministry is a two-way street. First we minister to an audience; second, and no less important, we minister to one another as participants. It is the latter activity that this section is concerned with.

It is a truism that ought to be remembered; the drama group that gets along together, performs well together—and the Spirit is able to use their work to His glory. Worship times have the potential to melt a gang of actors and technicians into a cohesive body, in which, according to the apostle Paul, "No person looks solely after his or her own interests, but after the group as a whole."

Be comfortable with the scripts in this section. The litanies can be helpful devices. They will plant thoughts and ideas into your participants' minds and hearts, that will surface later onstage or during times of testing.

The dramatic Communion service outline could be a satisfying experience for all involved. You may wish to bring your pastor in to officiate. However, if the rituals of your particular church allow, it could be a good experience for the group and its leader to be alone for this sacred experience.

Lillenas Drama

A Litany of Covenant

Appropriate to use at the start of a drama project.

LEADER: We serve a God who is creative; we pledge to serve Him through our human creativity.

GROUP: With God's help we will.

LEADER: Human creativity is to glorify God and not ourselves.

GROUP: With God's help we will remember this.

LEADER: Because God has given these gifts, we offer them back to Him as volunteers, committed to excellence.

GROUP: With God's help we will glorify Him.

LEADER: As Christians, we confess that God has created in Jesus Christ the perfect image of himself in human form.

GROUP: With God's help we will strive to be Christlike.

LEADER: We recognize the varied gifts of this group, coming together with one purpose, in the name of Jesus Christ.

GROUP: With God's help we will realize this purpose.

LEADER: To paraphrase the apostle Paul, "It was he who gave some to be apostles,

GROUP: some to be prophets,

LEADER: some to be evangelists,

GROUP: some to be pastors and teachers,

LEADER: some to be drama ministers,

ALL: so that the body of Christ may be built up."

A Litany of Beginnings

Based on Ecclesiastes 3

Appropriate for the first rehearsal

LEADER: There is a time for everything, and a season for every activity that awaits us in the preparation of this play.

ALL: A-men!

LEADER: A time to audition,

GROUP: and a time to get to work;

LEADER: a time to be punctual,

GROUP: and a time not to be late;

LEADER: a time to use script,

GROUP: and a time to be off book;

LEADER: a time to open your mouth,

GROUP: and a time to keep it shut;

LEADER: a time to enter,

GROUP: and a time to exit.

LEADER: A time to prepare.

GROUP: And a time to rest.

LEADER: A time for personal satisfaction.

GROUP: And a time for ministry.

LEADER: For us, drama is ministry.

ALL: A-men!

A Litany for the Green Room

We don't think there is a speck of green anywhere in the room in which we gather before a drama presentation, unless it's on the potato salad left over from last night's precurtain lunch. No one really knows how the term *Green Room* got started, but for the uninitiated, it's merely the place where the cast gets together before and during a play. For you it may be a Sunday School room just off the sanctuary platform; for the group we work with, the Green Room is a corner of the fellowship hall. Nonetheless, those minutes before a 10-minute sketch or a two-hour play can be stressful. Use the following short litany to draw the gang together and give them an energetic send-off to the stage.

LEADER: Thanks to hard work and the Lord's blessing,

GROUP: we are ready for this performance.

LEADER: Because the playwright has written an excellent script,

GROUP: we are ready for this performance.

LEADER: Inasmuch as the audience is anticipating our ministry,

GROUP: we are ready for this performance.

LEADER: As a culmination of our stewardship and God's faithfulness,

GROUP: we are ready for this performance.

LEADER: Because the Holy Spirit will use our words and actions,

GROUP: we are ready for this performance.

LEADER: When we step out onto that stage [platform], we will be . . .

GROUP: READY!

LEADER: We are ready for . . .

GROUP: THIS PERFORMANCE!

LEADER: And we will perform in the name of . . .

GROUP: CHRIST JESUS!

A Prayer for the Peace of God

Scripture: Philippians 4:4-9

Theme: Peace comes with acceptance of our gifts and trust in the God that has given them.

Cast: Leader, Reader 1, Reader 2, Group

There are many times in the course of a production, from auditions to the final curtain, when the concerns of life and our own vulnerability can seem overwhelming. Use this short passage from Paul's letter to the church at Philippi to remind the group that peace comes when we accept our gifts and trust God to empower us to use them effectively.

LEADER: Rejoice in the Lord always.

GROUP: I will say it again: Rejoice!

LEADER: Let your gentleness be evident to all.

GROUP: The Lord is near.

READER 1: Do not be anxious about anything, but in everything, by prayer and petition, with thanksgiving, present your requests to God.

READER 2: And the peace of God, which transcends all understanding, will guard your hearts and your minds in Christ Jesus.

LEADER: Finally, whatever is true,

GROUP: whatever is noble,

LEADER: whatever is right,

GROUP: whatever is pure,

LEADER: whatever is lovely,

GROUP: whatever is admirable—

LEADER: if anything is excellent or praiseworthy—whatever you have learned or received or heard from me, or seen in me—

GROUP: we will put it into practice.

LEADER: And the God of peace will be with you.

GROUP: And with you.

A Dramatic
Communion Celebration

Note: Most churches have a prescribed Communion ritual, and regulations as to who may serve the ordinance or sacrament. These may need to be taken into consideration when planning this devotional exercise. Portions or all of the following may be photocopied.

A Call to Celebrate the Lord's Supper

The Body of Christ is a special community made up of all who will declare Jesus as Lord. Within this community are groups of people who, because of common ministry goals, band together to learn, rehearse, pray, and find ways to carry out their ministry.

This group is such a community within the Body of Christ. We are united around the cause of Christian drama or theatre. To us, the craft is ministry, so, it is not usual for we of like minds to feel comfortable worshiping together, as well as rehearsing together. We have learned that rehearsals feed off of worship.

We have come together today [tonight] for a high and holy worship experience, the celebration of Communion [Lord's Supper]. Which in its original setting was indeed a dramatic event for a cast of 13, who were as varied and nondescript as the cast of characters here in this room.

The Gospel writers tell us that the stage upon which this foretelling drama was played out was an upper room, engaged by two of the major cast members, Peter and John. Its movement was blocked; part of which consisted of following a man carrying a jar of water into the building where the supper was to be held.

The transaction was scripted; the disciples were to say to the man, "The Teacher asks: Where is the guest room where I may eat the Passover with my disciples." Evidently all went according to the Director, who was Jesus himself. Luke's script reveals this bit of tech information, "They found things just as Jesus had told them. So they prepared the Passover."

Preparation for the Lord's Supper

Now, let us prepare for Communion by reading the following lines. *[You may want to plan for meditative music during this quiet time.]*

**Here, O My Lord,
I See Thee**

Here, O my Lord, I see Thee face to face;
Here would I touch and handle things unseen;
Here grasp with firmer hand eternal grace,
And all my weariness upon Thee lean.

Too soon we rise; the symbols disappear.
The feast, tho' not the love, is past and done.
Gone are the bread and wine but You are here,
Nearer than ever, still by Shield and Sun.

—Horatius Bonar

Psalm 84:11

The Lord God is a sun and shield: the Lord will give grace and glory: no good thing will he withhold from them who walk uprightly.

The Lord's Supper from Luke and John

LEADER: When the hour came, Jesus and his apostles reclined at the table. And he said to them,

MEN: I have eagerly desired to eat the Passover with you before I suffer.

GROUP: Before he suffers?

LEADER: The hour has come for the Son of Man to be glorified.

WOMEN: I tell you the truth, unless a kernel of wheat falls to the ground and dies, it remains only a single seed.

LEADER: But if it dies, it produces seeds.

MEN: The man who loves his life

GROUP: will lose it,

WOMEN: while the man who hates his life in this world

GROUP: will keep it for eternal life.

[You may pause here to allow participants to express personal words.]

LEADER: Jesus took bread, gave thanks and broke it, and gave it to them, saying,

GROUP: "This is my body given for you; do this in remembrance of me."

LEADER: Jesus said, "The Son of Man must be lifted up."

MEN: You are going to have the light just a little while longer.

GROUP: Walk while you have the light.

MEN: Before darkness overtakes you.

WOMEN: Put your trust in the light

MEN: while you still have it,

GROUP: so that you may become sons of light.

LEADER: This is my body, which shall be lifted up.

[Invite participants to pray brief prayers of thanksgiving. Distribute and partake of the bread according to your custom.]

LEADER: In the same way, after the supper he took the cup saying,

GROUP: This cup is the new covenant in my blood, which is poured out for you.

LEADER: Then Jesus said, a new command I give you:

MEN: Love one another.

GROUP: Love one another.

The Disciples' Prayer

Scripture: Matthew 6:9-13

Theme: The prayer we know as the Lord's Prayer is the prayer of intimate and committed Kingdom disciples. It works just as well for disciples in drama ministry.

LEADER: Merciful Father,

RESPONSE: Hallowed be your name.

LEADER: You are one God,

RESPONSE: the Father of us all.

LEADER: We trust you with our lives.

RESPONSE: We are your children.

LEADER: Your kingdom come,

RESPONSE: on earth as it is in heaven,

LEADER: your will be done,

RESPONSE: on earth as it is in heaven.

LEADER: Forgive us our sins.

RESPONSE: You are a merciful God.

LEADER: Help us to forgive others.

RESPONSE: We will be merciful.

LEADER: Father, protect us

RESPONSE: from yielding to temptation.

LEADER: Father, deliver us

RESPONSE: from the power of evil.

LEADER: We trust you with our lives.

RESPONSE: We are your children.

LEADER: Father, yours is the kingdom and the power and the glory forever.

RESPONSE: Amen.

Acts of Worship:

Scripture Arrangements

Scripture was created to be spoken. Whether the inspired originator was a prophet, Moses, a New Testament Epistle writer, or Jesus himself, the Word was probably heard, before it was read from manuscript.

That has something to say about the use of spoken Scripture in a worship service. Even though many of the hymns we sing at church are based on God's written word, the average noninvolved church attender will never know it. However, an opportunity for participation in the reading of Scripture will make an impression on the guest, that unknown choruses will never elicit. Use the following scripts with the group often. Write your own. Secure a copy of *The Word in Worship*, by Miller and Wyatt. It, too, is a Lillenas drama resource.

The Hope of Salvation

Scripture: Luke 1:46-55; Psalm 80:1-7

Theme: The Magnificat. Mary's prayer for her unborn child echoes our own hope and trust as we anticipate the celebration of Christ's birth and His eventual return.

Cast: Leader, Reader 1, Reader 2, Group

LEADER: Hear us, O Shepherd of Israel, you who led Joseph like a flock;

GROUP: awaken your might,

LEADER: you who sit enthroned between the cherubim, shine forth before Ephraim, Benjamin and Manasseh.

GROUP: Come and save us.

LEADER: Restore us, O God; make your face shine upon us,

GROUP: that we may be saved.

LEADER: And Mary said:

READER 1: My soul glorifies the Lord and my spirit rejoices in God my Savior, for he has been mindful of the humble state of his servant.

READER 2: From now on all generations will call me blessed, for the Mighty One has done great things for me—

GROUP: Holy is his name.

LEADER: His mercy extends to those who fear him,

GROUP: from generation to generation.

READER 1: He has performed mighty deeds with his arm;

READER 2: he has scattered those who are proud in their inmost thoughts,

LEADER: he has brought down rulers from their thrones

GROUP: but has lifted up the humble.

LEADER: He has filled the hungry with good things

GROUP: but has sent the rich away empty.

READER 1: He has helped his servant Israel remembering to be merciful to Abraham and his descendants forever,

READER 2: even as he said to our fathers.

LEADER: O LORD God Almighty, how long will your anger smolder against the prayers of your people?

READER 1: You have fed them with the bread of tears;

READER 2: you have made them drink tears by the bowlful.

READER 1: You have made us a source of contention to our neighbors,

87

READER 2: and our enemies mock us.

LEADER: Restore us, O God; make your face shine upon us,

GROUP: that we may be saved.

The Sign of Immanuel

Scripture: Psalm 24:1-7; Isaiah 7:14; Matthew 1:18-25

Theme: The birth of Christ

Cast: Leader, Reader 1, Reader 2, Group

LEADER: The earth is the LORD's,

GROUP: and everything in it.

LEADER: The world is the LORD's,

GROUP: and all who live in it;

READER 1: for the Lord founded the world upon the seas

READER 2: and established it upon the waters.

READER 1: In the book of the prophet Isaiah, it is written: "Therefore the Lord himself will give you a sign: The virgin will be with child and will give birth to a son, and will call him Immanuel.

GROUP: God with us."

LEADER: This is how the birth of Jesus Christ came about:

READER 1: His mother Mary was pledged to be married to Joseph, but before they came together, she was found to be with child through the Holy Spirit.

READER 2: Because Joseph her husband was a righteous man and did not want to expose her to public disgrace, he had in mind to divorce her quietly.

READER 1: But after he had considered this, an angel of the Lord appeared to him in a dream and said, "Joseph son of David, do not be afraid to take Mary home as your wife, because what is conceived in her is from the Holy Spirit. She will give birth to a son, and you are to give him the name Jesus, because he will save his people from their sins."

GROUP: The prophecy was fulfilled.

READER 2: When Joseph woke up, he did what the angel of the Lord had commanded him and took Mary home as his wife. But he had no union with her until she gave birth to a son.

LEADER: And he gave him the name Jesus.

GROUP: Who may ascend the hill of the LORD?

READER 1: He who has clean hands and a pure heart.

GROUP: Who may stand in his holy place?

READER 2: He who does not lift up his soul to an idol or swear by what is false.

READER 1: He will receive blessing from the LORD,

READER 2: and vindication from God his Savior.

LEADER: Such is the generation of those who seek him, who seek your face, O God of Jacob.

READER 1: Lift up your heads, O you gates;

READER 2: be lifted up, you ancient doors,

LEADER: that the King of glory may come in.

GROUP: Come, Lord Jesus. Amen.

This Is My Son

Scripture: Matthew 17:1-2, 5-8; Philippians 3:10-11; Psalm 99

Theme: The Transfiguration. Christ is revealed to the disciples.

Cast: Leader, Reader 1, Reader 2, Reader 3, Group

LEADER: The LORD reigns, let the nations tremble;

GROUP: he is holy.

READER 1: After six days Jesus took with him Peter, James and John the brother of James, and led them up on a high mountain by themselves.

READER 2: There he was transfigured before them. His face shone like a sun, and his clothes became as white as the light . . . a bright cloud enveloped them, and a voice from the cloud said, "This is my Son, whom I love; with him I am well pleased. Listen to him!"

READER 3: When the disciples heard this, they fell to the ground and were overcome by fear.

READER 2: Jesus came and touched them, saying, "Get up and do not be afraid."

READER 1: And when they looked up, they saw no one except Jesus himself alone.

READER 3: In the Epistle to the church at Philippi, Paul writes, "I want to know Christ and the power of his resurrection and the fellowship of sharing in his sufferings, becoming like him in his death, and so, somehow, to attain to the resurrection from the dead."

LEADER: Exalt the LORD our God and worship at his footstool;

GROUP: he is holy.

READER 1: Moses and Aaron were among his priests . . .

READER 2: They called on the LORD and he answered them.

READER 1: He spoke to them from the pillar of cloud;

READER 2: they kept his statutes and the decrees he gave them.

LEADER: O LORD, our God, you answered them.

GROUP: You were to them a forgiving God.

LEADER: Exalt the LORD our God.

GROUP: The LORD our God is holy.

LEADER: Worship at his holy mountain,

GROUP: for the LORD our God is holy.

In His Strength We Are Saved

Scripture: Matthew 4:1-11; Romans 5:20*b*-21; Psalm 51:1-2, 10-12

Theme: We cannot save ourselves. Through Christ alone we are saved.

Cast: Leader, Reader 1, Reader 2, Group

Leader: Have mercy on us, O God,

Group: according to your unfailing love;

Leader: according to your great compassion,

Group: blot out our transgressions.

Leader: Wash away all our iniquity,

Group: and cleanse us from our sin.

Reader 1: Then Jesus was led up by the Spirit into the desert to be tempted by the devil. After fasting forty days and forty nights, he was hungry.

Reader 2: The tempter came to him and said, "If you are the Son of God, tell these stones to become bread."

Reader 1: Jesus answered, "It is written: 'Man does not live on bread alone, but on every word that comes from the mouth of God.'"

Reader 2: Then the devil took him to the holy city and had him stand on the highest point of the temple. "If you are the Son of God," he said, "throw yourself down. For it is written: 'He will command his angels concerning you, and they will lift you up in their hands, so that you will not strike your foot against a stone.'"

Reader 1: Jesus answered him, "It is also written; 'Do not put the Lord your God to the test.'"

Reader 2: Again, the devil took him up to a very high mountain and showed him all the kingdoms of the world and their splendor. "All this I will give you," he said, "if you will bow down and worship me."

Reader 1: Jesus said to him, "Away from me, Satan! For it is written, 'Worship the Lord your God, and serve him only.'"

Reader 2: Then the devil left him, and angels came and attended him.

Group: Christ alone has conquered the power of evil.

Reader 1: In the Epistle to the Romans, Paul says, "Where sin increased, grace increased all the more, so that just as sin reigned in death, so also grace might reign through righteousness to bring eternal life through Jesus Christ our Lord."

Group: In his strength we are saved.

Leader: Create in us a pure heart, O God,

GROUP: and renew a steadfast spirit within us.

LEADER: Do not cast us from your presence,

GROUP: or take your Holy Spirit from us.

LEADER: Restore to us the joy of your salvation,

GROUP: and grant us a willing spirit, to sustain us.

At the Right Hand of the Father

Scripture: Luke 24:44-53; Ephesians 1:18-20; Psalm 47:1-6

Theme: The ascension of Christ. We can trust our lives to the God whose power is revealed in the resurrection and ascension of Christ.

Cast: Leader, Reader 1, Reader 2, Group

Leader: Clap your hands, all you nations; shout to God with cries of joy.

Group: How awesome is the LORD Most High!

Leader: He subdued nations under us, peoples under our feet.

Group: How awesome is the great King over all the earth!

Leader: Christ said to the disciples in Jerusalem:

Reader 1: "This is what I told you while I was still with you: Everything must be fulfilled that is written about me in the Law of Moses, the Prophets and the Psalms."

Reader 2: Then he opened their minds so they could understand the Scriptures.

Reader 1: He told them, "This is what is written: The Christ will suffer and rise from the dead on the third day, and repentance and forgiveness of sins will be preached in his name to all nations, beginning at Jerusalem.

Reader 2: You are witnesses of these things.

Reader 1: I am going to send you what my Father has promised; but stay in the city until you have been clothed with power from on high."

Reader 2: When he had led them out to the vicinity of Bethany, he lifted up his hands and blessed them.

Reader 1: While he was blessing them, he left them and was taken up into heaven.

Reader 2: Then they worshiped him and returned to Jerusalem with great joy.

Reader 1: And they stayed continually at the temple, praising God.

Reader 2: In the Epistle to the Ephesians, Paul writes: "I pray also that the eyes of your heart may be enlightened in order that you may know the hope to which God has called you, the riches of his glorious inheritance in the saints, and his incomparably great power for us who believe. That power is like the working of his mighty strength, which he exerted in Christ when he raised him from the dead and seated him at his right hand in the heavenly realms . . ."

LEADER: The Lord is risen.

GROUP: He is risen indeed.

LEADER: God has ascended amid shouts of joy;

GROUP: sing praises to God;

LEADER: the LORD has ascended amid the sounding of trumpets;

GROUP: sing praises;

LEADER: sing praises to our King;

GROUP: sing praises.

LEADER: For God is the King of all the earth;

GROUP: sing to him a psalm of praise.

LEADER: God reigns over the nations;

GROUP: God is seated on his holy throne.

LEADER: The nobles of the nations assemble as the people of the God of Abraham, for the kings of the earth belong to God;

GROUP: He is greatly exalted. Amen.

Light in the Darkness

Scripture: Psalm 27:1; Isaiah 60:1-3, 19-20; 1 John 1:5-7

Theme: God is our light when we are surrounded by darkness. Walk in that light.

Cast: Leader, Reader 1, Reader 2, Reader 3, Reader 4, Group

LEADER: The LORD is my light and my salvation—

GROUP: whom shall I fear?

LEADER: The LORD is the stronghold of my life—

GROUP: of whom shall I be afraid?

READER 1: Arise, shine, for your light has come,

READER 2: and the glory of the LORD rises upon you.

READER 3: See, darkness covers the earth and thick darkness is over the peoples,

READER 4: but the LORD rises upon you and his glory appears over you.

READER 1: Nations will come to your light,

READER 2: and kings to the brightness of your dawn.

READER 3: The sun will no more be your light by day, nor will the brightness of the moon shine on you,

READER 4: for the LORD will be your everlasting light, and your God will be your glory.

READER 1: Your sun will never set again,

READER 2: and your moon will wane no more;

READER 3: the LORD will be your everlasting light,

READER 4: and your days of sorrow will end.

LEADER: And our fellowship is with the Father and with his Son, Jesus Christ. This is the message we have heard from him and declare to you: God is light;

GROUP: in him there is no darkness at all.

LEADER: If we claim to have fellowship with him, yet walk in the darkness,

GROUP: we lie and do not live by the truth.

LEADER: But if we walk in the light, as he is in the light,

GROUP: we have fellowship with one another,

LEADER: and the blood of Jesus, his Son, purifies us from all sin.

In the Shadow of the Almighty

Scripture: Psalm 91

Theme: When fear overwhelms us, we can trust God to be our shelter.

Cast: Leader, Reader 1, Reader 2, Reader 3, Reader 4, Group

READER 1: He who dwells in the shelter of the Most High will rest in the shadow of the Almighty.

READER 2: I will say of the LORD, "He is my refuge and my fortress, my God, in whom I trust."

LEADER: Surely he will save you from the fowler's snare and from the deadly pestilence.

GROUP: The LORD is our refuge.

LEADER: He will cover you with his feathers, and under his wings you will find refuge.

GROUP: The Lord is our fortress.

LEADER: His faithfulness will be your shield and rampart.

GROUP: We trust in God.

READER 3: You will not fear the terror of night, nor the arrow that flies by day, nor the pestilence that stalks in the darkness, nor the plague that destroys at midday.

READER 4: A thousand may fall at your side, ten thousand at your right hand, but it will not come near you. You will only observe with your eyes and see the punishment of the wicked.

LEADER: If you make the Most High your dwelling—even the LORD, who is my refuge—then no harm will befall you, no disaster will come near your tent.

GROUP: The LORD is our refuge.

LEADER: For he will command his angels concerning you to guard you in all your ways; they will lift you up in their hands, so that you will not strike your foot against a stone.

GROUP: The LORD is my fortress.

LEADER: You will tread upon the lion and the cobra; you will trample the great lion and the serpent.

GROUP: We trust in God.

READER 1: "Because he loves me," says the LORD, "I will rescue him; I will protect him, for he acknowledges my name.

READER 2: He will call upon me, and I will answer him; I will be with him in trouble, I will deliver him and honor him. With long life will I satisfy him and show him my salvation."

Our Hope Is in the Lord

Scripture: Psalm 33:6-11, 16-22

Cast: Leader, Group

LEADER: For the word of the LORD is right and true;

GROUP: he is faithful in all he does.

LEADER: The LORD loves righteousness and justice;

GROUP: the earth is full of his unfailing love.

LEADER: By the word of the Lord were the heavens made, their starry host by the breath of his mouth.

GROUP: Let all the earth fear the LORD;

LEADER: he gathers the waters of the sea into jars; he puts the deep into storehouses.

GROUP: Let all the people of the world revere him.

LEADER: For he spoke,

GROUP: and it came to be;

LEADER: he commanded,

GROUP: and it stood firm.

LEADER: The LORD foils the plans of the nations; he thwarts the purposes of the peoples.

GROUP: But the plans of the LORD stand firm forever.

LEADER: No king is saved by the size of his army; no warrior escapes by his great strength.

GROUP: We fear the LORD!

LEADER: A horse is a vain hope for deliverance; despite all its great strength, it cannot save.

GROUP: We hope in the LORD!

LEADER: But the eyes of the LORD are on those who fear him, on those whose hope is his unfailing love, to deliver them from death and keep them alive in famine.

GROUP: Deliver us, O LORD!

LEADER: We wait in hope for the LORD:

GROUP: he is our help and shield.

LEADER: In him our heart rejoices,

GROUP: for we trust in his holy name.

LEADER: May your unfailing love rest upon us, O LORD,

GROUP: even as we put our hope in you.

Shout for Joy to the Lord

Scripture: Psalm 100

Cast: Leader, Group

LEADER: Shout for joy to the LORD, all the earth.

GROUP: The LORD is God.

LEADER: Worship the LORD with gladness; come before him with joyful songs.

GROUP: We are his people.

LEADER: It is he who made us, and we are his.

GROUP: We are the sheep of his pasture.

LEADER: Enter his gates with thanksgiving.

GROUP: Thanks be to the LORD Almighty.

LEADER: Enter his courts with praise;

GROUP: praise his name.

LEADER: For the LORD is good,

GROUP: his love endures forever;

LEADER: his faithfulness continues through all generations.

GROUP: Alleluia, Amen.

Ezekiel 36:22-32

(An Interpolation)

Cast: Leader, Male Reader, Female Reader, Men, Women, Group

LEADER: This is what the sovereign Lord says:

GROUP: I will show the holiness of my great name,

MEN: which has been profaned among the nations,

WOMEN: the name you have profaned among them.

GROUP: The nations will know that I am the Lord.

LEADER: These are the words of the sovereign Lord. He says, I show myself holy through you before their eyes.

MALE READER: I will sprinkle clean water on you,

GROUP: and we will be clean.

FEMALE READER: I will cleanse you from all your impurities,

GROUP: and from all our idols.

MALE READER: I will give you a new heart,

GROUP: and will put a new spirit in us;

FEMALE READER: I will remove from you your heart of stone,

GROUP: and will give us a heart of flesh.

LEADER: And I will put my Spirit in you and move you to follow my decrees and be careful to keep my laws.

MALE READER: You will live in the land I gave your forefathers;

FEMALE READER: you will be my people,

GROUP: and you will be our God.